RAISING PRIVATE CAPITAL

RAISING PRIVATE CAPITAL

Building Your Real Estate Empire
USING OTHER PEOPLE'S MONEY

MATT FAIRCLOTH

BiggerPockets® PUBLISHING

Raising Private Capital
Matt Faircloth

Published by BiggerPockets Publishing LLC, Denver, CO
Copyright © 2018 by Matt Faircloth.
All Rights Reserved.

Publisher's Cataloging-in-Publication data
Names: Faircloth, Matt, author.
Title: Raising private capital : building your real estate empire using other people's money / by Matt Faircloth.
Description: Includes bibliographical references. | Denver, CO : BiggerPockets Pub., 2018.
Identifiers: ISBN 978-1-947200-98-2 (pbk.) | 978-1-947200-04-3 (ebook) | LCCN 2018938234
Subjects: LCSH Real estate investment. | Real estate investment--Finance. | Mortgages. | Mortgage loans. | Venture capital. | BISAC BUSINESS & ECONOMICS / Real Estate / General
Classification: LCC HD1375.F35 2018 | DDC 332.6/324--dc23

Published in the United States of America
10 9 8 7 6 5 4 3 2 1

Dedication

I dedicate this book to the person I dedicated my life to so many years ago. To my life partner, my best friend, and my love, my wife, Liz. There are just not enough words. Thank you for all that you are to me and to so many others.

TABLE OF CONTENTS

CHAPTER 3
THE DEAL PROVIDER 37

CHAPTER 4
THE CASH PROVIDER 64

CHAPTER 5
WHERE TO FIND CASH PROVIDERS..................... 86

CHAPTER 9
MANAGEMENT, EXITING, AND BEYOND 164

FOREWORD

by **Joe Fairless,**
Host of the *Best Real Estate Investing Advice Ever* Show

Remember the scary thing you did that one time? And after you did it, it wasn't so scary anymore.

It was something that took a lot of courage, but darn it, you did it, and thank goodness you did! Maybe it was buying your first property. Maybe it was swimming from the shallow to the deep end. Or maybe it was finally asking out that good lookin' guy or gal you'd always had your eye on.

We are not human beings. We are human becomings. And I believe life is about how we continue to evolve through our experiences, using these experiences to continue to become a better version of ourselves so we can maximize our time on earth.

Take a moment to think about that scary experience you ultimately faced but worked up your nerve to push through and overcome. After you went through with it, I know for a fact at least these two things happened:

1. It opened up a new world of possibilities for you.
2. You didn't die. (Phew!)

Whether or not the experience ultimately worked out how you intended is another story, right? Sometimes we take a leap into something and it doesn't initially work out. But that's OK as long as we learn and grow from that experience and then apply those lessons to optimize future results.

So this raises the question, Why don't we jump into the deep end more often? If it opens up new possibilities for us, then why not always look for a deeper and deeper pool to do cannonballs in? Well, if we go diving in the deep end of a pool without first knowing how to swim, then that's going to be an issue. An issue for us and an issue for everyone around us.

Welcome to *Raising Private Capital: Building Your Real Estate Empire Using Other People's Money*. This book gives you the tools to learn how to properly raise money so you can grow your real estate empire while helping your passive investors achieve their financial goals. Without this book, raising money would be like doing a cannonball in the middle of the ocean during a tsunami. Not advisable.

So first, congrats on your purchase and your commitment to elevating your real estate game. But buyer, beware: With this book comes some serious responsibility. When you partner with passive investors, you are leveraging not just other people's money. You are leveraging their time. And time is the most precious resource we have. It is limited, and we can't get back what we lose. That is why Matt has put so much emphasis in this book on protecting private money. Capital preservation is the most important part of partnering with passive investors. First, the focus should be on return *of* capital. Then on return *on* capital.

I've interviewed investors during my podcast who have raised money from family members and lost it on a deal. Brothers and sisters didn't want to sit next to them at Thanksgiving. Lifelong friendships turned sour. We must avoid this by actively reading this book and applying its principles.

My suggestion to you as you read this game-changing book is to think about the dollars you raise from your passive investors in terms of time spent to acquire those dollars. Think about the time, effort, and sacrifices your passive investors undertook to earn that money that they are now going to trust you with in your deal. When we think about it in terms of time, not just money, it creates a clear picture of how important it is that we partner with investors only after we thoroughly understand how to protect their dollars.

After mastering that understanding and successfully partnering with passive investors, it's highly likely your real estate business will reach heights ten times faster than what you previously thought. I've seen this happen with my own company, Ashcroft Capital, and I've seen it happen with Matt's, the DeRosa Group. Matt and his wife, Liz, started with a $30,000 loan in Philadelphia in 2004. Fast-forward to today: They have completed more than $30 million in real estate transactions involving private capital. Think they would be where they are now if they had used just their own money?

The beauty of all of this is that the $30 million worth of transactions they've done represents so many passive investors whose lives they have positively affected by earning them a return that they likely wouldn't have gotten in other types of investments. Raising money is a win-win-win game. Residents win because you buy properties and improve the quality of life at those properties. Your investors win because you give them good returns. And you and your family win because you grow your real estate portfolio to the next level.

And if you choose to continue adding value to your investors and scaling your real estate empire, future generations can win as a result of your success. You can go from wanting to scale your real estate company to actually creating a legacy as the person who produced generational wealth for your family.

How cool would it be to have your primary financial focus move from whatever it is today to being focused on how to create wealth for your kids' kids' kids?

It's all possible as long as you follow the guidelines set forth in this book. Just remember, regardless of the types of challenges you will undoubtedly face along your journey, you can choose to use them as lessons to springboard you to the next level. The thought of raising money can be scary at first, but just as we talked about earlier, scary things, when acted on, open up a brand-new world of possibilities for you.

Good luck, and congratulations again on buying this book. Now, let's get into it.

INTRODUCTION

Let me start by saying that I commend you for looking to expand your real estate business and raise your game by bringing in private capital. I know of no better way to exponentially expand a real estate business than to bring in eager and willing investors to win alongside you as you grow.

This book is intended to be a road map for real estate investors who are looking to take their business to the next level by injecting more private capital into their business. I will explain the step-by-step process to acquiring, securing, and protecting private money. This book will teach investors how to look into their current network for potential private money partners. It will also teach them how to provide a win-win proposition to money partners, all while building the real estate investor's own business. I will discuss the specific roles in a deal: the person providing the deal and the person providing the cash and how they both benefit. I will go into deep discussion on how to work with your money partners and what types of deals will best benefit them based on their goals and the source of their capital. Most important, I will discuss how to protect you and your investor as you structure deals and how to unwind things when you are done.

This book will be full of stories from my personal experience because I've lived it. I've borrowed and lent money, completed fix-and-flips, bought apartment buildings, executed the Buy, Renovate, Rent, Refinance, Repeat (BRRRR) method. You name it, I've done it. I've made plenty of money using private capital. And you can too. There is nothing secret or unique about how I did it. I was not born with a silver spoon in my mouth, and I don't think it takes a certain background or a country club membership to be successful at raising private capital. It takes just the right tools applied in the correct manner.

I won't pull any punches in this book. This book will be light and funny when it needs to be, serious when appropriate, and full of stories and lessons I've learned along the way. I've had some big wins in this business, and this business has kicked my teeth in a few times. I will tell you about both ends of the spectrum, the wins and the losses. Through all my experiences, I have learned a certain equation that works in finding, enrolling, and implementing money partners into a real estate business. I will share that equation with you here.

The main reason I wrote this book is that I believe that real estate investors can provide a truly alternative investment to those who are looking for a way to build their wealth. I respect the stock market, but I believe that it can no longer be relied on as the sole vehicle to achieving wealth by retirement in this country. People need other investment options, and real estate investors armed with the right tools can offer true alternatives to the stock market while providing security and opportunity for growth long term.

Above all else, my hope is to inspire and educate you. I hope the material in this book will teach you to successfully and responsibly raise private money so that you can build your real estate investing business and achieve your financial goals. I want to help you get what you really want out of real estate investing so that you leave a legacy for your family and lead the life that success in this business makes available.

So let's get started.

CHAPTER 1
INTRODUCTION TO PRIVATE CAPITAL

Let's start at the very beginning ... What is private capital? People have different understandings of it, and there are various definitions and nuances of this term out there in the real estate investing world. For this book, we will define it as follows:

> *Private capital is a source of money that comes from an individual, not a bank or other financial institution. It is positioned in two ways, as a loan (debt) or ownership (equity).*

It's important to define this up front so that we are on the same page. There are a few things that private capital is *not* and won't be treated as such in this book. The first on the "not" list is a loan from a bank or other financial institution. It perhaps goes without saying that a bank loan isn't private capital, but the same goes for other sources of loans from financial institutions, like credit cards and business lines of credit. These can be good sources of money if they are handled properly, but they don't qualify as private capital.

The next is hard money lenders or other financial institutions that are in the "business of lending money." These are companies that do offer loans and equity on real estate deals. The difference is, they are most likely not lending their own money. They have their own investors and have to pay a return to them while also making a profit for themselves. For that reason, interest rates and fees can be higher than they would be if you were dealing directly with the investor. These lenders are also probably not flexible on their rates and terms, which is something you want to consider when dealing with true private capital.

You may get a hard money lender to agree to provide money as equity by giving it a percentage of the upside of the project, at which point it would be viewed as private capital, but I would be very careful in these circumstances. These institutions are used to lending their money at high interest rates with lots of fees and will want a large percentage of your project to achieve the same rate of return on their money.

The last source that I would disqualify as private capital is similar to a hard money lender, but the money is coming from an individual who is a professional money lender. This person is lending his or her money, but the rate and terms are more similar to those of hard money, and they're typically not negotiable. If you've been around the real estate investing world long enough, you've met these professional lenders. I worked with one lender who had a chain of record stores all around New Jersey and Pennsylvania. He saw the market changing with the advent of the iPod, sold all his stores, and was then lending his money to real estate projects. While I give him credit for being a good businessman, his rates weren't that different from hard money rates and included points and fees on top, just as a hard money lender would do. Don't get these folks confused with private capital.

Unique Factors of Private Capital

There are a few differentiating factors from the sources mentioned previously to the ones we will discuss in this book. In my eyes, private capital has three characteristics that make it unique.

DIFFERENTIATOR NO. 1 | Negotiability

Have you ever asked a bank whether you can defer the interest payments until the end of the loan? How about asking hard money lenders whether they would consider waiving a significant amount of their fees? You may be able to make this happen if you are a repeat customer of theirs, but odds are you are going to receive a big *no* on that request. If they do work with you, I predict that their flexibility will be minor and that they will still do their best to overprotect themselves from the downside of risk.

A private capital partner will most likely work with you and be open to back-and-forth negotiations. The reason for this is that it's *their* money. If you are borrowing from a bank or other source, the people you are dealing with are not putting their own cash into the deal, so their hands are tied. They are limited by either banking laws or lending standards that they must adhere to, and that's because they are playing poker with someone else's chips, and that someone has already told them what terms they are allowed to lend at.

This is not so for a private capital partner. It's their money, so they can work with you to come up with loan terms that work for you both. If you want to pay the interest at the end of the loan or negotiate a lower rate, ask for it. If you don't want to pay points or a fee if you need to extend the loan, ask for it. Because it's their money, they can say yes or negotiate until you come up with something that works for you both.

DIFFERENTIATOR NO. 2 | Win-Win

Banks' and other lenders' primary goal is to turn a profit for their organization. I know that most want to see you also succeed, but meeting their lending and profit goals for their organization is far and away their number one priority. That said, you can't work with them to show how alternative terms are just as favorable. Their hands are tied, so even if you have a solution that makes them more money, such as offering a small chunk of the profit on a fix-and-flip as part of their return, they can't do it.

A private capital provider is all about win-win. In this book, I will teach you how the more you win as a real estate investor, the more they win as your source of capital. They become tied to your success, creating a true strategic partnership.

DIFFERENTIATOR NO. 3 | The Source of the Money

As I said before, banks and other financial institutions are playing with someone else's money. That money belongs to either Wall Street or the Federal Reserve or, in the case of hard money lenders, their investors. They are getting the money at a cheaper rate, marking it up, and selling it to you. They make their money on the markup and the fees in originating that loan or equity in your deal.

Private capital providers are giving you their money, which came from either their retirement account or their own pocket. The more capital you give back to them with a return, the more they win and feel inclined to invest again and again with you on future deals, and the more their long-term wealth grows. As a side note, they could be getting the money from a real estate loan, like a home equity line of credit (HELOC), which is somewhat similar to a bank's position, but we will get there later in this book.

In my eyes, there are two very specific parties in a private capital transaction. They both have their roles, responsibilities, and risks they take on in the deal. I have terms I use for these two roles that will be used throughout this book: the Deal Provider and the Cash Provider.

Introduction to the Deal Provider

The Deal Provider is the one who goes out and finds opportunities such as fix-and-flips, rental rehabs, and other real estate investments that require an investment using private capital. The Deal Provider is also the one who is willing to put in the sweat equity to make the deal happen. This may include building a brand and reputation in the marketplace, finding and negotiating the purchase, dealing with banks, hiring and managing contractors and supervising vendor relationships, and dealing with real estate agents on the purchase (and sale) of flips. Deal Providers are the center of all the action of the deal and handle 99.999 percent of the "doing" that needs to happen. Deal Providers may also put in their own cash, or they can earn their share of the deal strictly through sweat equity. We will get into what it takes to be a great Deal Provider to your investors later in this book.

Introduction to the Cash Provider

The Cash Provider is the investor or lender of the private capital for the project. Most of the time, Cash Providers are passive investors making a return on their money. They have little or no active involvement in the deal aside from properly vetting it and the Deal Provider before making the investment.

A word of caution to my budding Deal Providers reading this book: Be careful of the willing Cash Provider who wants to have an active role in the project. I send my investors regular updates on our progress and allow them to walk my jobsites. I also make it clear who the operator of the project is and who is making the day-to-day decisions. Make sure that your Cash Providers trust you to make decisions on their behalf and work in their best interest without having a say in the day-to-day operations. If they have an issue with this, my bet is that they will slow down progress on your projects or, even worse, try to shut your deal down if they don't agree with a decision you make. We will get into many factors of Cash Providers in this book, including how to find those who truly want to be "passive" investors.

Private Capital Uses

Now that we are clear on what private capital is (and isn't), let's talk about how to put private capital to work in your business. Next I will review the different uses for private capital in a real estate business and how each use benefits the Cash and Deal Providers, along with the risks. In a later chapter, we will get into how to structure these types of deals and create win-win situations for both sides.

USE NO. 1 | Real Estate Debt

This is the most common use of private capital and perhaps the one most sought-after by investors. Quite simply, this is a loan to the Deal Provider from the Cash Provider. The loan is secured by a mortgage or lien on a specific piece of real estate. The Cash Provider agrees to put in a certain amount of cash, and the Deal Provider agrees to loan terms defined in the written loan agreements. If these written loan agreements are not met, the Cash Provider can come to take the real estate. The right that the Cash Provider has to come to take the real estate is called collateral. Collateral is security for the Cash Provider, and it answers the question, "What if you don't pay me back?" If the deal is fairly structured, the real estate that Cash Providers have a claim to is worth more than their loan amount, so if they do need to take it from the Deal Providers, they can sell it and get their loan proceeds. We will get into how to structure these loan agreements in a manner that's fair to both sides in a later chapter.

The terms of the agreement are defined in a promissory note and a mortgage agreement (some states call this second document a deed of trust). The loan generates an interest payment due to the Cash Providers, which is their main profit on their investment. The amount of this interest payment and all other loan terms are defined in the loan documents.

Benefits to the Deal Provider	Benefits to the Cash Provider
Cash Provider might be willing to lend *all* the project costs for the right deal.	Return is a fixed interest rate.
Terms like when the interest is due and the rate are negotiable.	Collateral provides security.
For short-term deals, you can borrow the money over and over again.	For certain sources of cash, these deals can provide exponential growth.
Risks to the Deal Provider	**Risks to the Cash Provider**
Time is a deal killer. The longer a project takes, the more you lose.	If the value of the property is less than the loan amount, there will not be enough collateral.
If things go off budget or over time, the Cash Provider can take the real estate.	Taking the real estate back can take a lot of time in some states.

USE NO. 2 ∎ Equity

Real estate equity is the most misunderstood tool to use in financing transactions, but it can be the most creative. Equity is ownership, either in the real estate itself or in the company that owns the real estate. It's a claim to the profits that are made and a responsibility to support the losses if they come up. In my experience, these types of deals are attractive to more savvy Cash Providers who think that the Deal Provider is making lots of money on the project, and they want in on the action. The arrangement between the Cash and Deal Providers can be complex, like a syndication on a large commercial or apartment project. These deals may involve the Securities and Exchange Commission (SEC) because selling an interest in your company to people who have no active role can be viewed as selling a security. This isn't a showstopper, but arrangement of these types of deals can be expensive. It could also be much simpler. We have given a small chunk of profits on our fix-and-flips to our Cash Providers as an incentive to get into a deal, and we have formed a small limited liability company (LLC) with one or two silent partners to go out and buy some single-family homes or small multifamily properties. The main things that need to be clear on both sides are the roles, goals, and compensation. Here are some questions that need to be answered in each of these areas:

1. **Roles** – Who will find the deals, supervise the renovations if necessary, manage the property manager on a rental deal, manage the construction and selling process on a flip, and handle all the financial accounting? Most likely, the Deal Provider will do all these tasks, but it needs to

be clearly defined. What are the expectations of the Cash Provider? Will the Cash Provider need to personally guarantee a mortgage if needed? Does he or she have any management responsibilities?

2. **Goals** – On a flip, when will the renovations be completed, and what is the target sale date? On a rental, when will the property be stabilized with solid tenants? When will it be refinanced? What are other timeline goals that need to be established? What are the profit and return on investment (ROI) goals? What are milestones and challenges we know of that stand between us and those goals?

3. **Compensation** – How much ownership does each party have? This is usually expressed as a percentage. Does that percentage apply to all profits, such as rental cash flow and sales proceeds? Does the Deal Provider get any fees, such as compensation for construction or property management, finding the deal, or hitting profit targets? Does the Cash Provider get a return on his or her money in an interest rate or a percentage of the profit or both?

All these questions need to be answered to be successful in these deals. It all needs to be laid out on the table with nothing assumed. The mantra you should have for equity deals is: "If it's not in writing, it didn't happen." That means that *everything* needs to be in writing to avoid confusion because confusion in real estate deals can land you in court—or worse. Make sure that you have a solid operating agreement or joint venture agreement that's been reviewed by an attorney. This chart sums up the benefits and the risks to both sides for real estate debt:

Benefits to the Deal Provider	Benefits to the Cash Provider
Exposure to more sophisticated investors.	Opportunity to share in the upside of a project.
Capacity to do larger deals.	Tax advantages.

Risks to the Deal Provider	Risks to the Cash Provider
Working with Cash Providers who think they bring more to the table than they actually do.	Picking the wrong Deal Provider (think Bernie Madoff).
Inadvertently breaking an SEC regulation.	Project loses money, leaving Cash Provider to have to put in more money to keep things going.

USE NO. 3 | Unsecured Lines

An unsecured line is a fancy way of saying loan. This loan doesn't have collateral as real estate debt does; it's just a loan from the Cash Provider to the Deal Provider. There is a large amount of trust involved in these types of loans, as Cash Providers have no real security for their loan. Sure, they could sue the Deal Provider, get a lien, try to convert that lien to a claim against the real estate owned by the Deal Provider, foreclose on that real estate, etc., but this can take a very long time, and the Deal Provider can easily hide behind LLCs or file for bankruptcy to make the claim go away. These loans are a major benefit to the Deal Provider and a leap of faith for the Cash Provider.

All that said, these types of loans do have their place and can be a win-win for both sides. The real win for Cash Providers is making a return on their money while helping someone they are close to get their business off the ground. I will never forget those who believed in us when we got started and gave us these types of loans, based not on the deals we were doing but on their faith in my wife and me.

These arrangements are typically between close friends or family members, but you still need to treat them as business arrangements. There should still be some sort of documentation to protect both sides (mostly the Cash Provider) and define things like the interest rate and payback terms. A simple promissory note will do, but it should not be overlooked.

Benefits to the Deal Provider	Benefits to the Cash Provider
Unsecured cash that can be used for start-up costs, down payments, or marketing.	Earning an interest rate on his or her money.
No ties to credit score or business track record.	There are no other benefits. Any other arrangement such as sharing in future profits or ownership should be viewed as equity.
Risks to the Deal Provider	**Risks to the Cash Provider**
Not being able to pay back the line and having nothing to give the Cash Provider as collateral.	Not getting paid back.
Loan is not attached to a property (there is no reliable cash flow to pay the interest).	No collateral to take if the loan is not paid back.

Final Thoughts on Private Capital Uses

Each of the three uses I outlined has many derivations and possibilities. They all have benefits and risks for you and your Cash Providers, and sometimes it might not be clear how to structure your deals. It's imperative to look at several different scenarios for each deal. Most important, you need to make the goals of the Cash Provider a top priority as you assess the different scenarios. We do a deep dive in later chapters on deal structure and aligning with Cash Providers' goals to set you up for success.

Sources of Private Capital

We've covered what private money is and isn't, who uses and provides it, and ways that it can be applied in your business. I've introduced you to the Deal Provider and the Cash Provider. Now let's talk about where the cash comes from—the actual sources of private money. Understanding these sources clearly will help you find Cash Providers in your network. My hope is that you get so proficient at identifying these sources that you are able to approach potential Cash Providers and show them capital they didn't realize they had (capital they can invest with you).

SOURCE NO. 1 | Cash

This one sounds like the most obvious, but it's sometimes the one that's hardest to find. When I talk about cash, I'm talking about free liquid money that's in a checking or savings account and ready to move. The Cash Provider could be a big saver who squirreled it away over many years. That one is hard to identify because people who are big savers tend to live below their means. They don't drive flashy cars or live in big houses; it may be quite the opposite. There is a book called *The Millionaire Next Door*, by Thomas J. Stanley and William D. Danko, that examines the lifestyles and spending habits of real-life millionaires. It's worth a read. You may think that the millionaire is the one with the huge house and a sports car in the driveway, but the millionaire may also live a low-key lifestyle.

For instance, one of my repeat investors is a retired widow. She lives in the same house she has lived in for the past 40 years, and it's paid off. She travels a few times a year but doesn't live too lavishly. She has some investments that produce fixed income for her and also collects Social Security. The advantage she has is that her expenses are low, so her income greatly exceeds them. She has an extra $40,000 or $50,000 a year left after everything is paid and has been putting that money into apartment-building syndications and private loans with us for years. If you met her on the street or saw her lifestyle, you would have no idea that she's a millionaire.

SOURCE NO. 2 | Real Estate

Real estate is one of the best sources of equity waiting to be unlocked. If you have your own portfolio of properties, you should be constantly looking at interest rates and the value of your properties versus what you owe on them. If you can pull some cash out and maintain the monthly payments with your rental income, it can be an easy way to unlock that equity and put that money to work in your own deals. The best part is that the money you pull out is tax-free because you are essentially borrowing it from yourself.

Cash Providers can also step in and pull equity from real estate they own to put into your deals. I saw online that 29 percent of the homes in America are owned free and clear,[1] with no mortgage debt on them. That's approximately one out of three. There are pretty good odds that someone in your immediate circle owns his or her home free and clear, which means that person is sitting on a pile of untapped equity that could be put to work to earn additional cash flow for them and build their wealth.

For example, one of our very first loans from a private lender was from a family member who owned her home free and clear. She wasn't doing anything with that equity, so she agreed to become a personal guarantor for a business equity line for our company. That allowed the bank to use her free-and-clear house as collateral. It takes an extreme amount of trust to get a family member to pledge his or her home for you to grow your business, and we didn't take it lightly. That said, it gave us access to capital to get started when it was hard to get a bank to take us seriously on our own.

SOURCE NO. 3 | The Market

When I say "the market," I am talking about anyplace in which people park money in hopes that it will grow, typically in a publicly traded platform like the stock market. It could be held in shares of a company like Microsoft (equity) or in municipal or corporate bonds (debt). It may be something that they can sell tomorrow and get their cash back, or it could be in something that's not liquid or has a major penalty if they want their cash, like a 401(k) or an IRA. Accessing retirement funds to put to work in real estate deals has been one of the best win-win arrangements in my business, and it can be for yours as well. I will get into the logistics of how to use an IRA of one of your investors to create these win-wins in a later chapter.

---

[1] https://www.zillow.com/research/free-and-clear-american-mortgages-3681

Final Thoughts

This chapter covered the basics of private money. For those of you just getting started, I hope it was beneficial and exposed you to some new terms and ways to look at how to integrate other people's money into your real estate business. For those of you who have been in the game for a while, don't forget that your investors are most likely new to this as well. It pays to remind yourself of the basics so that you can easily explain them to eager investors who are in need of education before they are comfortable getting started with you.

So now that we've gotten clear on the definitions around private capital and laid our foundation, we can start talking about what it takes to build a business that will create those win-win situations between the Deal Provider and the Cash Provider.

CHAPTER 2
PREREQUISITES BEFORE YOU START RAISING MONEY

I started real estate investing with house hacking my first real estate invest-ment, which occurs when you purchase a multiunit property, live in one unit, and rent out the others. I bought the three-bedroom, single-family home for $150,000 with a mortgage with 3 percent down and a monthly payment of $940 per month. I rented out two rooms to friends of mine who gladly paid me $500 each per month, which was slightly below the market. I was cash-flow-ing $60 per month and living there free, which was a great deal because I was still working full-time. Within two years, I had paid down all my credit card debt and paid off all my student loans. I was hooked.

My wife, Liz (who was actually my girlfriend at the time), and I really wanted to expand our real estate investments, so we approached her father for a loan of $30,000 (unsecured line of credit), which enabled us to buy a second rental property in Philadelphia. We bought a duplex in an emerging part of the city for $140,000 with one unit vacant and one unit occupied. We got our hands-on education right away, as we had to evict the tenant living in the property. We ended up turning the property around and leasing both units, with solid cash flow for several years. This was in the early 2000s, so the market was increasing nicely, which enabled us to sell it for a good profit a few years later.

I should pause here and say that I don't recommend that all of you go out and start buying real estate with the person you are dating and borrow the money from his or her parents. That could have gone in a very different direction. Liz and I were very clear on what we wanted out of life, and that included a five-year plan that we wrote together. We also wrote a promissory note to her father for that loan to protect both of us.

We got married in 2005 soon after we purchased that duplex. Part of our five-year plan was for me to quit my job and for us to live off her income alone so that I could build our business. That required us to live below our means and be very mindful of our expenses. None of that would have happened had Liz and I not been on the same page with our five-year goals and what we were willing to do for them to come to fruition. We made a few bad moves but also a few good ones, one of which was selling that duplex in Philadelphia and doing a 1031 exchange—in which an investor can sell a property, reinvest the proceeds in a new property, and defer capital gains taxes—for a small apartment complex consisting of eight units. We purchased some more rentals and refinanced others that had seasoned a bit, which gave us access to more capital to grow. Then the real estate market crashed in 2008, which left us holding the bag on a few fix-and-flips. We converted those to rentals because they wouldn't sell at a profit anymore. We were out of cash, and since the market was down, we couldn't refinance our way to more capital.

It was now 2010. We had spent the past few years waiting for things to pick back up and stabilizing our portfolio by finding solid tenants, improving our management, and lowering expenses where we could. We hadn't bought a deal in a few years at this point, but we had systematized our business and were ready to move beyond our stunted growth to reach our goals. We just needed capital, since our own funds and close-family resources had been tapped out.

In this same year that our business had plateaued, I met two key Cash Providers who, over the following seven years of investing, allowed us to grow our portfolio *ten times over.* The first Cash Provider we worked with was Liz's graduate school friend. She was catching up with him over coffee during a visit to New York City and told him about what we were up to. His ears perked up when he heard we were investing in real estate, and he said the key phrase: *"I would love to invest in real estate, but I just don't have the time."* He and I had coffee soon after, and we agreed to do a small equity deal together. We formed an LLC and bought a few single-family homes. He was willing to put in $50,000 as equity, and I would do the legwork to borrow the rest and get the houses renovated, leased, and refinanced.

I had a second Cash Provider lined up who had done some real estate transactions using his colleague's self-directed IRA as a loan. He had done well working as a Deal Provider and built up a small portfolio of rentals for himself using the BRRRR method with the IRA capital. He saw the power of leverage that his lender was able to use and wanted to do the same with his own IRA. He also needed to focus his time on his full-time job and was willing to step out of the doing and be a passive investor, using his own IRA to fund our deals. We struck a deal on rate and terms, and he lent Liz's friend and me the rest of the money to buy two single-family homes and renovate them.

I will talk more about these two Cash Providers later in the book. However, I wanted to share with you how I got started, how it did not happen overnight, and when in my career I began raising private money (outside of family). From 2003 to 2010, I was laying the groundwork as a real estate investor so that I would be in the position to handle private money partners. I am not saying it should take you that long, but I do think prerequisites are critical if you want to be taken seriously in this business and be in this business for the long game.

Why Can't I Start Raising Money Now?

Would you put your life into the hands of a pilot on his first day in the cockpit of an airplane? Of course you wouldn't. You would be foolish to do that. How about investing with a financial planner who has no experience, training, or knowledge of wealth-building strategies? You would be foolish to do that also, of course. The same goes for us real estate investors. When presenting a deal, you are asking your potential Cash Providers to put their financial futures into your hands when they invest with you. You owe it to them to have your act together so that you can be a trustworthy steward of their money. I know that we live in a world of instant gratification, especially for my younger readers out there who want to reach financial freedom by next Tuesday. I love your enthusiasm, but you need to know that real estate investing is a marathon, not a sprint. To be truly successful in this business, you will need to spend dedicated time preparing before you get started with private money. I can tell you that your growth will be exponential if you take the right steps first and don't just jump in and figure it out. You can do that, and you may even get some people to invest with you. But without the right tools, you won't grow very fast, and you may even step into pitfalls that you could have avoided had you properly prepared yourself.

Not to scare you with analogies that may take you back to your high school or college days, but there are some prerequisites to raising private money that I'll lay out for you. You don't need to do them in any particular order, but the more proficient you are in these four areas, the better off you will be when you start going out and raising money for your deals.

PREREQUISITE NO. 1 | Get Educated

First and foremost, a successful business owner never stops learning, so if you plan on being successful, plan on continuing to learn throughout your entire career. My most successful friends read a book or more a month. There is an adage that "leaders are readers," and I've found this to be 100 percent true. There are so many great real estate and foundational business books out there for you to choose from. If you gain one concept that will better your business from each book and commit to apply it moving forward, it's worth it.

When Liz and I got started, we took an entire year to become educated before we bought our first property. We attended countless local real estate meetings and took as many courses as we could on the subject of real estate investing. We read books together and talked about how to apply what we were learning to our future business. It gave us a solid foundation of knowledge and best practices to build from, and today I still use many of those strategies we learned.

Another way you can get educated is to consider taking the classes that real estate agents take to get licensed. Those classes will teach you every aspect of the real estate transaction and help you build your network if you take the classes in person. Once you complete the coursework, you can consider getting your real estate license for some additional income while you build your real estate investment business. Some of the most successful real estate investors I know started out as agents and slowly built their portfolio of rentals until they had enough income to stop agency work and invest full-time.

Specifically, here are some foundational areas of the business that I think are necessary for you to get educated in if you are going to be successful.

The Real Estate Transaction – Learn every aspect of buying and selling property, and the language that is associated with real estate transactions, so that you can clearly and competently communicate with agents and other professionals you will need to work with.

Negotiation Skills – These are invaluable skills that will aid you in getting good deals, building contractor, vendor, and partner relationships, as well as determining terms and conditions with your Cash Providers. If you don't feel as if negotiation is a strong suit for you, there are some tremendous courses that you can take to sharpen these skills. Regardless, this is one skill that you will need to have to be a successful Deal Provider.

Accounting and Finance – For you folks out there who aren't numbers people, the bad news is that the real estate investment business is full of numbers. It's a numbers- and accounting-based business, so you need to learn to read, understand, and create financial statements for your deals.

PREREQUISITE NO. 2 | Develop a Track Record

Beyond the textbook and theoretical education, you also need to get your hands into this business and learn by doing. Would you ever teach your child to ride a bike just by reading them a book about it? While that might be a great way to introduce the topic and get them comfortable with the idea of riding a bike, your child will need to physically get on a bike to *really* learn how to ride. Learning a concept on paper is one thing, but applying it in the field during a real estate transaction will ingrain it into your memory forever.

Once you build your educational foundation, you can go out and begin investing with your own capital (if you have it). This is the easiest path and the one I highly recommend, if it's possible for you. Potential Cash Providers will like to see that you put your money at risk in this business ahead of theirs. If you don't have your own capital to get started with, you will need to get exposure to real estate deals with the following activities, none of which requires much monetary investment (or requires less than the capital needed for a deal):

Become a Real Estate Agent

This option works well for many people I've watched grow over the years. If you hang your license with the right company, you can make enough money as an agent to manage your personal expenses while you build your investing business. If you come across a great deal, take your Realtor hat off and put your investor hat on. Additionally, you should find a few trustworthy real estate investors to take on as clients and see whether they will allow you to witness and be a part of every aspect of their transaction. Document every step in the process and what you learn along the way.

Become a Wholesaler

I can't speak too much on the nuts and bolts of wholesaling because I am not a wholesaler. However, I have worked with wholesalers closely for years. In essence, a wholesaler gets a deal under agreement (contract) with a seller and then assigns his or her position in that contract to an investor for an assignment fee. It's a good way to get started, meet other investors, and make a few dollars while you are at it. The trick is that wholesaling can be a full-time business by itself. It takes money and time to market for deals. You will need to make a decision at some point: Do you want to be a full-time wholesaler and ramp up that side of the business, or are you doing it as a stepping-stone to get into being a landlord and flipping?

Become a Project or Property Manager

There is no better way to get hands-on experience and learn the landlord or flipping business than by being a project or property manager. You will experience firsthand the day-to-day activities—the good, the bad, and the ugly. More important, you will get to learn while working on someone else's rental or flip project. This is so important because, in essence, he or she will be paying you, which in turn means that you will get paid to learn. If you find landlords or flippers who are still doing a lot of the day-to-day activities themselves but are on a growth spurt, pitch them on doing this work for them to help them grow while they help you learn. This arrangement can be a really good win-win scenario.

Find a Mentor

Another option is to find a mentor (a more experienced investor) and become his or her mentee. Mentors can be invaluable, as they can keep you out of trouble with their perspective and experience. They can help you avoid the mistakes they made themselves or repeat their wins by using the same formula they used.

One of the best ways to find a mentor is to seek out someone (or a company) you want to emulate who is investing in the exact type of investment vehicles you are interested in. You want to find the investor you want to be "when you grow up." Once you find a mentor, figure out how to add tremendous value to his or her business. So many people approach me and, before learning about our business and/or how they can help, begin the conversation with "Can you be my mentor?" Instead, first learn about potential mentors' business, goals, and focus areas. Then go to them with ideas on how you can add value to their business. All seasoned investors have tasks that they wish they could off-load on someone else—whether it is social media related, property management related, or office related. Additionally, every single seasoned investor is looking to grow in two areas: finding money and finding deals. Figure out how you can add value by helping investors find money (to put deals together) and find deals (to invest their money). If you can do this, they will want to do whatever they can to help you.

A Mentee Who Turned into a Business Partner

A few years ago, I was mentoring a couple of new investors on expanding their business. One of my students did very well during the program and even made some offers on a few multifamily deals. He and I stayed in contact after the program completed, having regular calls and mentorship conversations. Eventually he found a larger deal and asked me to step in as his mentor on the deal in exchange for some equity. I would audit all his documents and his underwriting and give him as many contacts as I could to ensure his success. He would be the driver on the deal and would call me when he needed my help. We agreed on a small slice of the equity and the asset management fee as compensation. This arrangement is a win-win for the mentor and the student. The student gets to keep the lion's share of the profit and does the majority of the legwork. The mentor is there when needed, with a role of helping the student be successful through the deal, watching his or her back, and opening up the Rolodex of contacts to the student. So far, it's been a great arrangement. I foresee us doing many deals together in the future. Bottom line: Whom in your network could you approach with an arrangement like this?

Regardless of which path you take to develop a track record, it's important to keep a running document of every real estate investment deal you have interacted with. What did you do on the transaction? What were the results? Did the project achieve its ROI/profit targets? Why or why not? What did you learn? Compile all this data into a track record document, which will summarize the deals you have done and the highlights for each deal. It will benefit you greatly when you sit down with your first Cash Provider and show him or her the experience you've gained in this business, what you've learned, and the profits/ROI you've helped create.

PREREQUISITE NO. 3 ▌Take a Personal Inventory

When I say "take a personal inventory," I mean take a look at what you bring to the table first. What do you possess that will benefit your Cash Providers? Why would these individuals choose you over some other real estate investor? What makes *you* a unique investment? What are your strengths and weaknesses? Don't ever forget that although you may have a smoking-hot deal that will produce a great return, the primary thing that a Cash Provider will want to vet out is *you*. Here are the key "personal inventory" areas that I invite you to assess and/or gain clarity on for yourself.

Time – It is imperative to become clear on how much time you can put toward real estate investing. Many of our Cash Providers like the fact that we are full-time real estate investors. We are always there if they have a question or even want to walk a property. I am not saying you have to be full-time; however, you need to be clear with yourself and your potential Cash Providers regarding the time you do have to put into your real estate investing business.

Money – If you are looking for private money, many potential Cash Providers will want to know whether you are going to put in money (whether you are going to have some skin in the game). Some real estate investors will tell you that they don't put any of their own money into a deal, and other investors will tell you that they do put in money along with the Cash Provider. Regardless, the key is to be clear on your personal financial position. What personal resources and/or assets do you have the potential to use? Don't let the answer to this question stop you. You can be successful whether or not you have money to invest.

Once you have an answer for this, you will then need to establish how much private money you are looking for. One of the best things we have done with most of our private money deals is to use them to purchase and rehab the property (either for buy-hold or buy-flip). In other words, this has allowed us to do cash deals and then refinance once the project is complete (sold or rented). The deal moves faster this way, which makes everyone happy.

Skills – What are your skills? What are your strengths? Every single person reading this book (and in this world, for that matter) has skills. Each of us is great—even excellent—at something. The key is to identify your strengths and then figure out how to translate these skills and strengths for the real estate investing world. The good news is that many skills are transferable. For example, say you have strong analytical skills, and you have gained these skills from many years of working in the auto industry. Well, this skill (even though it is from another industry) could be hugely beneficial when analyzing real estate deals.

The first step is to gain clarity on your strengths and skills. Then you can determine your gaps (skills that you need that you don't possess). You can deal with these gaps by learning the skill yourself, by developing a team, or even by forming partnerships.

Your "Why" – This one is fairly simple and straightforward. You need to become crystal clear (and honest) with the reasons (and motivation) you are investing in real estate. I invite you to go deeper than simply "making money." This is not deep enough. There are so many different ways to make money in this world. You need to be able to answer: *Why do I choose real estate investing as a vehicle to make money?* Every Cash Provider needs to trust his or her investor. You build trust by sharing your goals and reasons for getting into real estate investing with people. You also build trust by being as authentic and transparent as possible with your Cash Providers.

Your Goals – I see so many new investors who just want to jump in and take action. Their motto is "Any deal will do as long as it's a real estate deal." The problem is, they don't have a clear set of goals to follow, so they don't really know where they are going. They are like a ship without a compass. They may discover a treasure, or they may end up sinking, and both are likely. You need to set some short- and long-term goals, mostly for your own benefit to keep yourself focused and on track. I recommend setting goals in the following increments: one year, three years, and five years. This will give you some short- and long-range plans to strive for. It will also benefit your potential Cash Providers because they'll be able to see where you are going and where they will go if they decide to start funding your projects.

PREREQUISITE NO. 4 | Create a Business Plan

The last prerequisite is developing a solid business plan to take what you have learned and put it into action to manifest your goals. There are hundreds of templates out there for business planning. One of the best models is from the book *The One Page Business Plan* by Jim Horan. I can remember the day as if it were yesterday when we filled out Jim Horan's one-page business plan template and, as a result, our company, the DeRosa Group, was born. Having a strong business plan in place will help guide your actions and activities, since it is very easy to get distracted in this business. Besides creating your vision and mission, your business plan should consist of three aspects: a strategy, a market analysis, and a team.

Strategy – So now that you have your goals set, how are you going to get there? Will you be doing fix-and-flip projects, rentals, or both? What types of properties will you be going after? How will you finance these transactions, and what is your target profit for each deal? What is your role in this strategy and plan? What are specific action plans that you can follow to achieve your goals and objectives?

Market Analysis – If you are looking to invest in Albuquerque, you'd better know that market like the back of your hand if you are going to make a good impression on your potential Cash Providers. If your strategy includes buying and holding, what are investors buying properties for in that market? What is market rent? What is a good deal? What amenities does the typical renter look for? Who are your typical renters? What is the prospective cash flow that can be expected for a market rate deal? If your strategy includes buying and flipping, what are the types of homes buyers want? Is it a strong buyer's market? What is the average sales price for a nicely renovated home? Consider other factors like major employers, current job market, median income, crime rate, and school system.

Team – No real estate investor I know acts alone. It takes a team to be successful in this business. Depending on your real estate investing niche, your team members will vary. However, here are some key team members that most real estate investors have: wholesalers, investor-friendly real estate agents, bankers, a CPA who specializes in real estate, an attorney, reliable contractors and general contractors, an insurance agent, a title agent, and a property management company. Not only will these team members help you run an effective business, but building a strong team will show a potential Cash Provider that you have done your homework and have a network of people who can help you reach your goals.

Now it's time to take inventory on these prerequisites. When you begin to evaluate yourself in each of these areas, make sure you assess where you are currently and where you want to go.

- **Prerequisite No. 1** – Get educated (real estate transactions, negotiation, accounting and finance).
- **Prerequisite No. 2** – Develop a track record.
- **Prerequisite No. 3** – Take a personal inventory (time, money, skills, your "why," your goals).
- **Prerequisite No. 4** – Create a business plan (strategy, market analysis, team).

Once you have taken inventory on yourself, it's time to compile everything. I suggest that you take everything from prerequisites one through three and create a résumé for yourself. It should powerfully state who you are, where you have been, what you bring to the table, and where you want to go. That, along with the business plan described in prerequisite four, will provide you with a solid presentation to put in front of a potential Cash Provider. If you take the creation of this seriously, you will have a concrete road map for yourself and a real case for why you are a great investment for any Cash Provider.

CHAPTER 3
THE DEAL PROVIDER

Now that we've learned all about private money, its sources, and what you need to do before you go out and start doing deals, let's talk more about your role as the Deal Provider. As the Deal Provider, you are the assembler of opportunities. You provide short-term and/or long-term investment opportunities to your Cash Providers. You search and analyze deals. Then you take the best ones and present them to your Cash Providers. You are providing them with opportunities to build their wealth, and in today's market, they need alternatives to the mainstream options. Through investments with you, they can double their retirement account balance regardless of what Wall Street is doing (we will do a deep dive on how to use retirement accounts as investment vehicles in the next chapter). They can also build streams of passive income for themselves that will pay out for years to come. All as a result of working with you.

A true Deal Provider is viewed as someone who can make things happen in other circles as well. Once you become proficient at pulling together capital for opportunities, Realtors and wholesalers will remember that you are a serious buyer and will bring their strong deals to you first. If you play your cards right, you will be viewed as one of the key players in your market by other investors, and the word will get out that you make things happen. Once you get to that place, it's just a matter of keeping enough money partners lined up to take on the opportunities you're presented with. A solid Deal Provider is standing in the center of the action, getting a first look at the best deals and the first call when someone with money wants to put it to work in real estate.

You might be wondering why we haven't started talking about specific real estate deals yet, and I can tell you that while the deal itself is very important to the Cash Provider, it's not the most important thing. *You*, the Deal Provider, are the most important factor. Since you will be the person injecting his or her funds into the deal, Cash Providers need to know that they can trust you with their money first.

Will you quit if things get tough?

Will you try to cheat them or cut corners if you can?

Are you connected with a solid network of people to help you reach your goals and bring projects to completion?

Are you committed to playing the long game or interested in making a quick buck?

All these questions and more will come up as you start presenting deals, which is why the first part of this chapter is dedicated to developing *you* as a well-equipped Deal Provider.

SYSTEMS | The Key to Success

If the scenario I just described sounds appealing to you, then consider what can happen if your business overheats, things start to happen quickly, and you get a solid reputation as a deal closer and someone who can put capital to work for investors. I've seen real estate investors ramp up too quickly, saying yes to all the deals and all the money that come in the door. They end up imploding because they didn't set up systems to handle a high volume of business. Balls start getting dropped. It's not pretty, and it can get bad when other people's money is involved. Don't let this happen to you. I suggest you take a look at the one-, three-, and five-year goals you wrote down in the last chapter and think about what you can do to automate your business to reach those goals easily. There are so many systems out there to benefit property management, project management, financial management, time management, and investor relations. I am not going to get into too much detail about specific systems to implement (since that is beyond the scope of this book). However, I will strongly encourage you, after reading this book, to implement systems and processes for the following areas. All these areas will help you be an exceptional Deal Provider.

1. **Finding the Deal** – This can be one of the hardest jobs as the Deal Provider. You need a strong system, process, and team in place to help

you uncover opportunities (whether they are flips or rentals). I would highly recommend Anson Young's *Finding and Funding Great Deals.* Although we have been investing for a while, I still uncovered some great tips and strategies.

2. **Analyzing the Deal** – Not only do you have to become competent at analyzing deals, but you also need to become excellent at this skill. You need to create a process to analyze each opportunity, which should include using some sort of tool and/or BiggerPockets calculator. Even if an opportunity does not come to fruition and/or you don't present it to a potential Cash Provider, it is helpful to keep track of your potential deals to help aid in your learning and growth.

3. **Presenting the Deal** – I will get into this later in the book as well. However, this is an important step in the process. Sometimes you will have a more formal presentation such as a slide deck, and other times you will present the deal more informally. It depends on the type of investor, your relationship, and the complexity of the deal.

4. **Purchasing the Deal** – Getting to closing is always the fun part! If you are not an expert in this piece of the puzzle, work closely with an investor-friendly Realtor who is.

5. **Managing the Deal** – If you are managing a fix-and-flip, put a strong process in place for managing the contractor and finances. If you are managing a renovation of a rental, same idea goes. If you are managing a stable rental, ensure you put a strong property management system in place. We currently use AppFolio for our portfolio.

6. **Managing the Cash Providers** – I will get into this topic much later in the book, as well, but just know that this is indeed a process in and of itself. You worked so hard to gain an investor in your business; now you need to manage and cultivate that relationship.

Establishing the best system and process depends on your goals and the types of real estate deals you want to do. Since there are so many tools and apps out there in the market, your best bet is to check out BiggerPockets and read the forums about which tools and apps will help you achieve your specific goals.

Working from the Inside Out

One of the fastest ways to become a Deal Provider is to make investments in yourself. I'm going to go a little deep here, so go with me. Who you are and everything about you (your thoughts, your past, your outlook on the world, and your view of yourself) add up to equal your current situation in your life. And this certainly includes your satisfaction (or dissatisfaction) with that situation. It's easy to play the blame game. Isn't that game fun? However, it is not a very effective game. I have found that taking personal responsibility for all my circumstances is not always easy but absolutely necessary. Over the years, I have realized that just as I have the power to get myself into a tough situation, I also have the sole power to change my life for the better. To create real change in your life, you need to shed your current actions and thoughts that aren't serving your long-term and short-term goals. To live a bigger life, you need to learn how to be a bigger human being. Let me repeat that again because I really want you to hear this statement and take it in: *To live a bigger life, you need to learn how to be a bigger human being.*

If you really want to be a successful Deal Provider whom people are willing to trust with their life savings, their children's college funds, and their long-term wealth goals, you need to work on being the highest and best version of yourself. You might be saying to yourself, "How do I do this?"

Ask yourself (and be honest), "Looking at my day-to-day life, what gets in the way of my being the best version of myself?" Maybe it is a lack of confidence, judging yourself, being critical of others, avoiding conflict, or not keeping your word. Maybe you will find this answer easily and then work to improve it.

Liz and I are always working on ourselves, always sharpening the saw, as the late Stephen Covey described in his best-selling book from the 1990s, *The 7 Habits of Highly Effective People.* We have participated in many different types of personal development weekends and seminars, such as the Landmark Forum and the Millionaire Mind Intensive. I've done some men's retreats through an organization called MDI (Mentor Discover Inspire), Liz and I have done some couples retreats to work on our relationship, and we have also attended many real estate investing workshops and classes. Whether you find value from a book, a course, therapy, or everyday experiences, the key is to be incredibly aware of yourself. You need to become obsessed with continuously assessing what is working and what is not working. Never settle for average or the status quo. Commit yourself to becoming the best version of yourself, and you will find more and more private money partners who will want to work with you.

I will share with you, from firsthand experience, that this is easier said than done. However, it is a critical step in becoming a Deal Provider whom others can trust. You have to know yourself and your blind spots. For example, I realized early in my career that I am not an overly detail-oriented person. I would rather think macroscopically and focus on the big picture. I am great at seeing an opportunity, creating a solid plan on how to bring it to fruition, and then handing it off to a detailed person to turn the vision into reality. At times, I can get lost in the details, but I work with lots of people who don't. I've learned to surround myself with people who have different skill sets that complement my blind spots.

To continuously work from the *inside out*, you need to continuously be in the conversation of self-improvement. I highly recommend two specific strategies for you to implement, if you are not doing these already.

STRATEGY NO. 1 I Join (or Form) a Mastermind Group

To continue to "sharpen the saw," you need to be in the habit of being around like-minded and growth-oriented people. The concept of mastermind groups was formally introduced by Napoleon Hill, who wrote one of my favorite books, called *Think and Grow Rich,* in the early 1900s. My wife and I have been involved with mastermind groups for years and find tremendous value in them. Participants of mastermind groups challenge each other to create and implement goals, brainstorm ideas, support each other, and provide peer accountability. You can be involved with an in-person mastermind or, as my wife does, participate in a mastermind online, via Skype, for instance. If you can't find a mastermind, simply use the BiggerPockets forums to meet others and form your own group. This is a free way to surround yourself with like-minded and growth-oriented people.

STRATEGY NO. 2 I Continue, Start, and Stop

It is hard on a day-to-day basis to be always aware of yourself and aware of areas to improve. One habit I implement after almost every project is an exercise called "continue, start, and stop." This is a great exercise to do by yourself but even more powerful to do with a partner or a team. After a project, each person answers the question, "What should I continue doing, start doing, and stop doing?" Most people have a hard time with the stop component, so don't let your team or yourself skip this one. All people can think of ways to improve themselves, and implementing this exercise after each project completion will force you to assess what went right and what you and your team are going to do differently moving forward.

Getting Your Name Known

As a Deal Provider, you have to always be networking and building relationships. This is one of the most underrated skills of a real estate investor. You might think this is super easy for people, but it is not. It is hard work to foster, build, and maintain relationships. And this does not happen overnight. I have my own networking equation that has served me in the past. It's a three-step process:

Step No. 1 – Surround yourself with high-quality people who can help you reach your long-term goals.

Step No. 2 – Work hard to understand their long-term goals clearly.

Step No. 3 – Do your best to help them achieve their goals through introductions to people who can help them and resources they need to be successful.

If I effectively do steps one through three, those people will help me get where I want to go in return. There are two circles in particular that you need to participate in for your networking activities, and they are both important for different reasons.

CIRCLE NO. 1 | Real Estate Investors

Perhaps it goes without saying, but if you want to be a successful real estate investor, you may want to go and spend some time with ... real estate investors! Makes sense, right? Just make sure to pick the right circle of investors. Of course, my number one recommendation for real estate networking, both online and in person, is BiggerPockets.

Beyond BiggerPockets, there are other circles you can check out. Just be careful of the circles with high fees to join or the groups that invite gurus to speak. I find the best real estate networking groups are focused on information, mentorship, best practices, and experiences, taught by people who work full-time in the business.

In these types of networking groups, you have two goals. The first should be to find deals that suit your criteria for your goals—deals you can send out to your investor database once you have one. Remember, the more deals you complete in those circles, the more you will be known as someone who makes things happen. When that wholesaler has a deal that needs to close in two weeks, and he or she doesn't have time for someone to come along and get cold feet the day before closing, you want that person to call you. It pays to have integrity in these groups, so take up the opportunity to prove that you can deliver. If you say you can close in two weeks, make it happen. Even on a smaller scale, if you tell someone you are going to be somewhere at a certain time or deliver something on a certain day, then make sure you do it. If you are dealing with someone who can help you realize your goals, it will pay off big for you. Doing what you say you are going to do is the best way to get a first look at the best deals in your real estate network, prove yourself to potential Cash Providers, and establish relationships with strategic partners in the future.

Your second goal is to weed through the crowd and find the diamonds in the rough. Almost every real estate circle I've seen has them; you just need to look. The diamonds in the rough are Cash Providers and mentors. Cash Providers come to these circles at times to find deals to invest in. They don't want to get swarmed, so they won't announce that they want to be a passive investor in your deals, but if you get to know them and their goals, you will see how you can effectively help them get where they want to go by being their deal source. The second diamond in the rough is that seasoned investor who is willing to take you under his or her wing and help you out along the way as a mentor.

SUCCESS·TIP *Here's a big tip on how to be successful, especially for the new investors reading this. If you can, see whether you can help the meeting leader/organizer in some way. I would recommend that you build a relationship with the meeting leader. Take him or her out to lunch and ask how you can help. Every organization and/or meet-up group is always in need of help and support. Eventually, as you build this relationship with the meeting organizer and begin to add value to the group, your reputation will improve, and members will begin to trust you. This will help you get more exposure in the group, which will help you propagate the networking equation and reach goals one and two above.*

You may find that there is not a group in your area that suits your needs. In that case, don't be afraid to start one yourself. You can start small and build it up, and there are resources like Meetup.com and BiggerPockets to broadcast your meeting so that others in your area are aware of it. Odds are, if you are looking for a real estate networking group and it doesn't exist in your area, there are other people looking for one too.

CIRCLE NO. 2 | Other Business Networking Groups

Sometimes you have to get your head outside the real estate investing bubble to get a fresh perspective and round out your network. I have seen many real estate investors make the mistake of networking only with other investors, which will slant your contacts heavily.

To be a well-rounded investor and a super-connected Deal Provider, you need to get involved with some general business networking groups like BNI (Business Network International), LeTip, and other independent ones out there. Most of these groups function the same way. They meet a few times a month, typically in the early morning before the work hour starts. The meetings are mostly the same format: They have a speaker or two, and they exchange business leads for each other. There is typically a member from each area of business, most of which can benefit your business—a Realtor, a CPA, an attorney, a financial planner, an insurance agent, and a contractor. There will be others, as well, who may be able to help you. What makes these groups unique is that if there is already someone in the seat who covers a certain area of business, no one else in that field can join. That way, the members can refer their leads to the person in that seat with no conflict. It's a good system, as long as the members trust one another. The good news for you is that most real estate investors don't bother with these groups, so there is most likely a seat open for the "real estate investor" profession. If you find a group you like with quality people, take that seat, even if you are just getting started.

Once you are in a business networking group, your goals should be as follows. Your first goal is to find people you can help. The first inclination of most people who get involved with these groups is to find people who will help them. That is the wrong approach. Your goal is to build relationships. The best way to do this is to help others and add value to their businesses *first*. Your second goal is to meet people you can add to your team, like a quality CPA, banker, attorney, Realtor, contractor, etc. Your third goal is to educate your group on what you do and how they can help you grow your business. You need to share with them and make it clear that you are looking to build your potential investor database. Many of these professionals don't understand the real estate investing game, and it's your job to educate them on how individuals can build their wealth with safe, secure projects with you (more on how to line up those conversations later).

I have been involved with many of these types of groups over the years. The biggest mistake people make when they join these types of groups (or any type of networking group) is that they don't schedule one-on-one meetings with the other members. It is really hard to get to know everyone in these groups as a result of attending a weekly or bimonthly meeting. The real relationship building happens when you meet one-on-one with these other members and really get to know them and how you can help them achieve their goals. Yes, this approach takes more time and energy. However, it will pay off as you build your network. Also, if relationship building is not a natural skill of yours, I highly recommend Never Eat Alone *by Keith Ferrazzi and Tahl Raz. The book is full of useful tips and strategies for becoming more effective in networking and relationship building.*

Work Your Way to the Front

When you pick the circles inside and outside real estate that you want to affiliate yourself with, it's time to get to work and use the networking equation I gave you. You want to leverage those circles to help others achieve their goals and then ask for help in advancing your goals. That's phase one. Once you've gotten to know the players in the group, it's time for phase two. This phase is about being of value in the group and finding a way to volunteer. Ask to run the front desk, help set up, or clean up, if that's possible. Do whatever you can to add value. This might mean referring people you know to join, finding speakers, or finding sponsors. When an opportunity to take on a role as an officer in the group becomes available, take it. The more you are seen as someone who is committed to the long-term success of the group and willing to go the extra mile, the more people will trust you and eventually bring you leads for your business.

If you play your cards right, you will be given opportunities to get in front of the room. It could be moderating a panel, introducing a speaker, or reading announcements. Whatever it is, take it. The more you get your face in front of that room of people, the more they will remember you as an active player in the group. If you are lucky, you may get the opportunity to lead the group. I would strongly suggest that you take that opportunity if it comes your way.

I was the president of my BNI chapter for six months and also the leader of the local real estate club in my area for several years, and I can tell you that it made a tremendous impact on the growth of my business.

There are plenty of you reading this who are not natural public speakers, and that's OK, but you do need to become proficient at it to be a successful Deal Provider. Use these circles to sharpen your public speaking saw. As you grow as a Deal Provider, you will need to present your deals to Cash Providers, and may find yourself pitching one of your deals to a group of investors in public. You never know. Being a solid public speaker will benefit you in many areas of life, especially in your real estate investing business.

The Deal Provider's Investment Vehicles

Up to this point, we've talked about what a Deal Provider is and how you can set yourself up to be successful at it, but we haven't talked about a very crucial part of the equation, which is the deal you bring to the table. Here are three investment vehicles to consider, as well as risks and case studies.

VEHICLE NO. 1 | Fix-and-Flips

For those of you who are brand-new to real estate, have never used Bigger-Pockets, or have never watched any of those flipping shows on TV, you may not know what a fix-and-flip is. At its core, a fix-and-flip is a project in which an investor purchases a piece of property, renovates it to create an increase in its value, and then sells it to recoup that value. The majority of the time, these projects involve single-family homes, which are renovated and sold to people who will live in the home, also known as end buyers. The renovations can be small, such as sprucing up the kitchen, bathrooms, and flooring, and adding a fresh coat of paint. They can also be extensive, full-gut renovations. Building a new house from scratch is even considered an advanced level of fix-and-flip. Full-gut renovations and new construction deals should be reserved for the most experienced investors, but don't run from them if they come up. See whether you can enroll a more experienced investor to partner with or mentor you on the deal to keep you out of trouble.

Another type of fix-and-flip is a turnkey. A turnkey project involves a rental-grade property, single-family or multifamily, which is purchased, renovated, and sold to another investor who plans to hold it long term. The flipper will also put tenants in the property and will either manage it for the buyer as part of the sale or negotiate a contract with a property management company to run the asset for the buyer. Either way, a turnkey means an investor can "turn the key" at closing and start making a hands-off cash flow on the deal. Turnkeys can be real win-wins, as long as you have a good source of tenants and can structure management for the buyer, either by yourself or through a third-party manager.

The other type of fix-and-flip deal to mention is what I call a wholesale flip. This is a hybrid of wholesaling, which involves putting a deal under agreement with a seller and then assigning your position in that contract to an investor for an assignment fee. In wholesaling, typically the second investor is the one who actually closes on the deal to purchase it; the first investor just takes a fee for structuring the deal for investor number two. A wholesale flip, on the other hand, is when investor one actually closes on the deal, does little or no work to the property, and then resells it. Since investor one is the owner on title, he or she can list the property on the MLS (multiple listing service) through a real estate agent to get more exposure. These types of transactions work only when you buy the property for a great price to begin with and think the deal is actually worth a good bit more than what you paid in its current condition. These deals are risky, as you can get "stuck" with the property if no buyers come along. I recommend doing these deals only when you have a huge margin between your buy price and potential resale, and you need to plan to roll up your sleeves and renovate the property if it doesn't sell quickly.

We've done our share of fix-and-flips, but they are not my only investment vehicle, nor do I brand myself as a flipper. In today's economy, they make sense, and they are a good way for me to provide a solid return to my Cash Providers. As long as home sales stay high, we will continue to do them. When the market takes a dip, we will find other ways to make those chunks of cash and provide short-term investment vehicles to our Cash Providers. Remember, fix-and-flips are a vehicle for the Deal Provider also. While they provide a short-term investment with some collateral to your Cash Provider, they provide chunks of cash to the Deal Provider. The chunks of cash come at the end of the deal, when it sells, and can be very important to your growth. That money is high value as you grow your business because it can be used to fund new projects or pay off debt for deals that didn't go as well as planned. They can become seed capital for larger ventures or fund marketing efforts to elevate your brand so that more Cash Providers can help you.

Risks to Consider

Any investment has its potential risks, and fix-and-flips have plenty of them.

Regarding working with investors, it's pretty simple. The largest risk you take on a flip is not being able to return the investors' capital and interest when the deal is over. This can arise a few different ways. Perhaps your deal didn't sell for your target sell price because the market shifted while you were under construction. Maybe you had to fire your contractor halfway through the job and hire someone else, which drove up construction costs. What if something unforeseen comes up, like repairs you have to make to the house that you didn't anticipate? To boil it down even further, if you don't sell for your target number at the end or if you pay more than you thought you would have to during renovation, your flip can go under. The way to mitigate this risk is by being very conservative with your numbers. Don't project a sell price that's at the very top of the current market. Put in some contingency for just-in-case expenses that may arise during the project.

The other risk that can come up for some of the same reasons mentioned above is running out of money before the project is complete. I hate to say it, but I've been there. We have had to go into our own pocket to complete a project or take some of the profit from a winning flip to complete a flip project that's behind on its budget. There are so many unforeseen things in a flip, and you can't predict everything that's going to happen through the project. The way to mitigate this risk is to have backup cash set aside. Ideally you will have some reserves of your own; you should if you have completed a few projects already. You could also ask your Cash Providers to set aside a reserve of cash for you. You will go to them only if you absolutely need it to complete the flip. Cash Providers will gladly do this if you show them that this is the best way to ensure the project's success, which in turn returns their capital and interest to them.

SUCCESS·TIP *It's important that you don't live on the entire profit from a fix-and-flip, or not all the money anyway. You should peel off 30 percent of your profit for income tax at the end of the year and give another 30 percent to your business for growth, to keep your business financial house in order or to fund other projects that may need some additional cash. If you can manage to live on the remaining 40 percent of the profit, you will line yourself up for long-term success by keeping your business healthy first.*

FLIPPING CASE STUDY
Four-Bedroom, Two-Bath, Bucks County, Pennsylvania

One of the givebacks I do is volunteering at my church by working the sound booth. I was a little bored one Sunday, so I started surfing on Trulia to look for deals. I saw a new listing come up in a good part of Bucks County, Pennsylvania, just across the Delaware River from my office. From the listing photos, it looked as if the house needed a new kitchen, updated bathrooms, and new flooring—a typical fixer-upper. The asking price was $230,000, which was attractive because the market for a house this size in good condition was between $375,000 and $400,000. At that price, the house wasn't going to stick around on the market very long, so I emailed the listing to a Realtor I knew who was well connected in that market. She got right on it and set up a showing for my partner and me the very next day. As a side note, when you are farming an area for flips, find the Realtors who are most active in that market. You want to list your flips with the agents who are well known in those markets, produce tons of marketing, and know those areas well.

On the property tour, we saw that along with a kitchen and bath upgrade, the house needed a new HVAC system and a roof. The total renovation budget was $80,000. Even at full asking price, this house was a good deal. Another reason to use agents that are strong in the area you are targeting is that they know other agents well. My agent knew the listing agent on the house and was able to get the backstory for us. The house was occupied by an elderly woman who had recently passed away, and her son was now settling her estate. He didn't live in the area and was motivated to sell the house quickly. We decided to go in with a strong offer of full asking and a two-week closing.

The house had gone on the market three days earlier, and they already had ten showings and two offers. All the other interested parties were home buyers looking for a good deal and planning to fix the house up themselves. The problem with those types of buyers is that they require financing from a bank, which can take around sixty days to get to closing. Additionally, their offers are contingent on financing, meaning the buyer can cancel the agreement if they are not able to get a loan. Our offer was not contingent on our getting financing, which made us that much stronger. Our agent vouched for us, telling the seller's agent that we were a strong buyer and would close quickly.

Another side note here: A cash offer doesn't mean that you are actually closing with cash. It just means that you are waiving the financing contingency that would allow you to get out of the deal if you couldn't get a loan. It puts some pressure on you, as the buyer, and you'd better make sure you have a few options lined up before you make an offer like that.

Here is how I financed it. I had a cash investor who had done a few smaller deals with us to this point. He was more conservative and wanted to be in a first-position mortgage and wasn't comfortable financing construction. He did allow me to get a second mortgage from another investor, who was using an IRA. We agreed to borrow the money as needed from this lender, with him advancing money to us only when we hit our prearranged construction milestones. Both lenders agreed to an interest rate of 9 percent, payable when the house sold. Since the cost to purchase and renovate the house was so much less than its actual value, both lenders agreed to finance 100 percent of the purchase and renovation costs.

Purchase Price	$230,000
Construction Costs	$80,000
Closing Costs (purchase and sale)	$22,000
Carrying Costs (interest, real estate tax, insurance)	$14,000
Sale Price	$430,000
Profit	$84,000

VEHICLE NO. 2 ▌ Small Rentals

The next vehicle to consider is small rental properties. For those new to the game, I am defining a rental property as a piece of real estate that is leased out, with revenue coming in that exceeds the expenses and mortgage, thereby producing cash flow. Some would read this and ask, "What about properties that don't produce cash flow?" If you have not renovated the property yet but, once you do, anticipate it to cash-flow, it's a future rental. If the property is renovated and its income does not cover its expenses, then, no, that does not qualify. It's not producing cash flow in its improved state, which means it's costing you money each month, which is bad. I have seen some friends of mine buy these "rentals" in high-property-value areas and be willing to hold them long term and lose money each month in hopes that they will see future appreciation. I do understand that strategy, but I don't think it's sound investing; it's speculation. There is no telling how long you will have to hold a property like that before it will make you any money, and you are losing on opportunity cost for deals that can put money in your pocket in the way of cash flow today. I am a cash flow "now" investor and look for rental deals that make money once they are renovated. If I can increase rents over time and add value as we go, even better.

For the purpose of this conversation, we are going to define small rentals as between one and ten units. These units are most likely all residential homes or apartments but do sometimes have commercial on the first floor for mixed-use buildings. Cash Providers can be used on larger deals or ones with all commercial, office, or industrial space, but it gets more complicated. We will discuss that in the next section.

The most common strategy for small rentals is the BRRRR method. If you are active on BiggerPockets, you've heard of it, I'm sure. It's an acronym, which breaks down like this:

Buy – Find a dilapidated or underperforming property in an area with solid rental potential.

Renovate – Bring the property up to market expectations for a rental and up to code requirements.

Rent – Bring in tenants who have been properly screened with written leases to live in the property.

Refinance – Based on your new market value and rental income, refinance the property.

Repeat – If you play your cards right, you can repeat this process over and over and over.

The key is that when you buy, make sure you think about all the R's that are to follow. How much renovation does it need? What will the unit(s) rent for? Will that rent carry all the expenses? How much will it be worth when you're complete? Will a bank be willing to give you a refinance on this property based on its financial performance and its value in the market when you're complete? When you refinance, will you be able to get all your costs out so that you can repeat over and over?

Making a BRRRR project work is a symphony of market knowledge, construction management, banking relationships, and property management. Another key to this process is a solid Cash Provider. Most likely, you will not be able to get a bank loan on your initial purchase and construction costs, so you will need a Cash Provider to loan you the up-front capital if you don't have enough of your own cash. As I said, if you play your cards right, you will be able to get that Cash Provider's money out completely when you refinance and can borrow it again on the next deal and the next one and the next. I've even done a few deals in which I was able to pull out the Cash Provider's loan and then additional money on top for my business growth. On the other side, there have been times when I've had to bring money to closing to pay off the Cash Providers because the refinance loan didn't provide enough to pay them off completely. You need to prepare for both scenarios when doing the BRRRR strategy.

BRRRR works best for single-family homes for many reasons. They can be bought at a low discount when they are not in good condition, are easiest to renovate, and tend to rent and appraise for higher per unit than small multifamily properties. Additionally, it's easiest to find a dilapidated single-family to get started on versus a rundown five-unit that is discounted to the degree that the BRRRR strategy will work.

Another method for small rentals is to buy an already-performing property and improve it over time. This is more often the strategy for multifamily properties, as you can buy them based on today's performance and increase rents, reduce expenses, and slowly improve them as you go to increase their value. You most likely won't refinance them and pull out much capital, but you can increase your cash flow more and more each year and look to refinance or sell them years down the road.

Cash Providers can play a role in long-term rentals like this, but they need to be OK being in the deal long term with you. It's best to position them as equity, giving them a piece of the cash flow as you go along. Since the deal has rental income, a bank will most likely give you a loan based on that income, a loan with a lower rate than what a Cash Provider would want from you on the same deal.

Small rental deals give Cash Providers another secure place to lend you money with collateral if it's a loan, and a way to enjoy cash flow alongside you if they are positioned as equity. Deal Providers get to build their rental portfolio, which will be a small stream of cash flow at first but will grow into larger and larger checks each month as you grow your business. The biggest advantage that rentals give a Deal Provider is access to income that is not linked to time. When structured properly, a rental will produce checks for you each month whether you put effort into them that month or not. That enables you to go out and find more deals for your Cash Providers and grow your business further.

Risks to Consider

If your small rental project uses the BRRRR strategy, you run the same risks that fix-and-flips have regarding cost overruns. Additionally, you run the risk of your deal not appraising for your target number to get all your Cash Provider's capital out. Perhaps you purchase a property for $50,000, complete $60,000 in renovations, and budget for $10,000 in carrying costs for a total development cost of $120,000. You need an after-repair value of $160,000 or more for a refinanced loan at 75 percent loan to value to get all your investor capital out. What if your bank wants to do only 70 percent loan to value? What if the property appraises for $140,000? If your Cash Provider is a lender, you may need to pay the provider back the balance of the loan out of future cash flow on the property or go into your own pocket to pay the provider back. If your Cash Provider holds equity in the property with you, you may need to shift ownership in the provider's favor to cover him or her. It is important to discuss these what-ifs with your Cash Providers before going into the deal so they are prepared.

SUCCESS·TIP *These types of investments involve playing the long game. If a flip is a sprint, a buy-and-hold is a marathon, so make plans to stay in the race the whole time. After your renovation is complete, who will handle property management? For deals in which your Cash Provider has ownership alongside you, what is the exit strategy? To be successful in small rentals, be sure to have answers to the questions that may not come up today but will come up down the road during the life cycle of the investment.*

SMALL RENTAL CASE STUDY
Two-Unit, Mixed-Used Building, Trenton, New Jersey

Some investors don't do deals with storefronts. In some circumstances, I like these kinds of deals because the storefront operators tend to take very good care of the space and will do most of their maintenance themselves. The problem with buildings with storefronts is that they can be very hard to fill with a quality tenant who can afford to furnish it, pay employees, and handle the expenses while the business ramps up. It's all about the quality of the tenant in these buildings. They will either make or break the deal.

I had been approached by the owner of several barbershops in town. He was looking for another location to be run by his nephew, who had just graduated from cosmetology school. I told a local real estate agent of mine to be on the lookout for a mixed-use building in the prospective tenant's target area. A few months later, he approached me with a three-story building consisting of one two-bedroom apartment over a storefront that was a jewelry store until recently. The owner of the store was retiring and had closed up shop. His son was helping him unwind things and had the building up for sale. The neighborhood had changed over the years, and the site was no longer a good location for a jewelry store, but there was a very popular barbershop on the next block.

My business owner contact really liked this because he felt he and his nephew could ride on the coattails of the competitor's shop. He agreed to lease the shop from me if I would pay $10,000 toward the costs to build out the storefront to accommodate a barbershop. This is called fit-out costs, and it's common for the owner to pay for some of them for the right tenant who is willing to sign a long enough lease. This tenant was willing to pay market rent and was willing to sign a five-year lease with a 5 percent rent increase every year. It was a good deal for both of us. The residential unit was already occupied by a tenant who kept it in good condition and had lived there for ten years. He wanted to stay as long as we agreed to make some much-needed repairs to the property.

All of this added up to a good deal—I just needed to finance it. I had an investor who approached us looking to do some long-term equity partnerships. He had potential to do some really big deals with us but wanted to start with an investment of $50,000 to try us out. I also had another Cash Provider lined up as a lender with $40,000 in an IRA to put to work. I set up an LLC with the equity partner as 50 percent owner and gave the lender a mortgage for 12 percent, payable when the property refinanced. Everyone was happy, so we put the deal under agreement and got to work.

After renovations, the residential tenant gladly signed a new lease at market rents. The storefront owner put in charge his nephew, who fell on his face and quit the business within three months. Whoops. The uncle pulled out also, and my lease didn't have a personal guarantee in it, so they were both off the hook. I was left with a nicely renovated barbershop with equipment that now belonged to me. I went to another local Realtor who listed the property on the MLS for lease and was able to find another tenant in about a month at the same rent we had projected. The lesson learned here is to always have a backup plan and to have a really solid lease with a personal guarantee from the business owner.

Once we were fully leased and at market rents, I needed to take out the private lender we had in place. I went to a local bank that was glad to lend us enough money to take out the lender plus some of my equity partner's cash to use as operating capital on that deal. We were all set, but once the bank reviewed the operating agreement, they saw my 50 percent partner and wanted him to personally guarantee the mortgage. This got even more complicated because he was a doctor, and it's hard to get a doctor to put a signature on anything because of potential malpractice claims. I hadn't spoken to my bank ahead of time about how the refinance would get structured, which was another mistake on this deal. The bank wasn't willing to do the deal without a personal guarantee from all owners, and my Cash Provider wasn't willing to sign off on the loan. After a few conversations and going back and forth, we were able to transfer his ownership over to his wife, and she signed off on the loan. This worked for the bank also, but the lesson in this deal is to make sure you have your takeout loan lined up and know the responsibilities of your Cash Provider in the refinance, if any.

Purchase Price	$75,000
Renovation Costs	$20,000
Monthly Rental Income (when complete)	$950 (two-bedroom apartment) and $900 (store)
Appraised Value (when complete)	$150,000
Monthly Cash Flow	$650

VEHICLE NO. 3 ▍ Syndications and More Complex Deals

Although the fix-and-flip and the small rental are the most widely used vehicles in Deal/Cash Provider partnerships, there are more complex derivatives of these two. There are also quite a few vehicles that are more off the beaten path and typically used by specialists in a certain niche of real estate investing. Of course, there are too many of these derivatives and niches to discuss here, but I would like to review a few of the more common ones.

Introduction to Syndications

A syndication is really a rental deal on steroids. It involves a larger commercial property, usually an apartment complex or a strip center. A pool of Cash Providers are assembled and are typically given equity (ownership) in the deal in exchange for their investment. They typically have little or no involvement in the day-to-day operation of the deal, with all control given to the Deal Provider. In exchange for his or her work to find, negotiate, close, and manage the deal on behalf of the Cash Providers, the Deal Provider gets a slice of ownership, typically called a carve-out. There are plenty of moving parts to these deals, and we will get into how to structure them in a later chapter. What I really want to underscore here is that there are rules in setting up these deals, and they are regulated by the SEC. People have gone to jail for improperly operating these companies, and you *must* have an attorney involved in setting you up for compliance.

SYNDICATION DEAL CASE STUDY
Apartment Complex, Lancaster County, Pennsylvania

Purchase Price	$3,350,000
Equity Required	$1,050,000
Mortgage	$2,512,500 (75 percent Loan to Value)
CAP Rate at Purchase	7.2 percent
Equity Split	70 percent to Limited Partners (Cash Provider), 30 percent to General Partners (Deal Provider)
Investor IRR (Internal Rate of Return) for Project	13.5 percent
Number of Investors	17 (average investment, $61,000)
Largest Investment	$180,000 (smallest was $25,000)
Project Timeline	Five years

We had been doing larger and larger deals with our investors, most recently an eighteen-unit apartment building in Philadelphia. We self-managed that property with our in-house team and were doing very well with it. I had been building a following on our YouTube channel and had appeared on the BiggerPockets podcast with Liz. We were getting calls from potential Cash Providers showing interest in working with us, and our current investors were pleased with the returns they had gotten from us on the private loan projects and equity deals thus far. I sent out monthly newsletters to our current and prospective investors to keep them in the loop on what we were up to and to let them know about deals we had for investment.

I felt that we had the management experience and investor database to expand into larger properties, so we started looking for bigger deals. Philadelphia was getting more and more expensive, and I really liked what I was seeing from the Central Pennsylvania market. The cost of living there versus the average income in some towns created a very "affordable" environment, meaning that most people who lived in that area could easily afford the average cost of housing. You don't see that everywhere, and it's a good sign if you are a landlord of middle-of-the-road rentals because it increases the likelihood of rents being paid on time. I put my feelers out in that marketplace through a national broker who focused on investments, the same one who had sold us the eighteen-unit in Philadelphia. He sent me deals, and I always sent him feedback, even if I wasn't interested.

Eventually, he sent me something worth looking into. It was an apartment complex (less than one hundred doors) that was converted from a factory in Lancaster County. The location was great, with a train station across the street and a short walk to the downtown area, which had several retail shops and restaurants. Since the complex was a converted factory, the units had an industrial feel, with spiral staircases, exposed brick, spiral ducts, and large windows. I liked a lot of the aspects of the deal, so I went out for a tour.

I met my agent and the owner at the property and saw the opportunity right away. Most units were in good condition, but the property was not being optimally managed. The owner had been managing it himself with some help from one of the tenants and a family member. There were five vacancies, and given the location of the building, there didn't seem to be a reason why he couldn't fill the vacant units. I asked the owner how he was marketing his vacant units, and he pointed to a small For Rent sign at the front of the complex with a phone number on it. A family member was the only one doing maintenance and turning over the vacant units. This took several months, considering the ongoing maintenance on the property and the fact that the family member had a full-time job. Additionally, the rents were around 15 percent below market based on my research. Everywhere I turned, I saw opportunities for optimization through better management systems. The problem was that, just like many deals on the market these days, the property was overpriced. They were asking $3,900,000, while our numbers showed that the deal made sense between $3,200,000 and $3,400,000. The broker and I had mutual respect for each other, as we had closed a deal in the past, so I told him our price range. He laughed and told me that was way too low and that everything he had on the market was selling close to asking. Another buyer ended up putting the deal under agreement for $3,800,000 soon after, and I put the deal behind me.

About two months later, I got a frantic call from the broker. Apparently, the buyer dragged them out for a few months and then backed out of the deal. When the other buyer backed out, the owner told the broker that he needed to sell quickly because his mortgage was coming due soon. He hadn't told the agent about the loan maturity date until now, believe it or not. The owner had only three months to either sell or refinance the property before the mortgage went into default. He also had a partner on the deal who really wanted his investment back. The broker told the owner that the only other buyer he trusted to close the deal was me, and we were at a much lower offer. The broker expected the owner to laugh when he heard our offer, but when he told his client that we were between $3,200,000 and $3,400,000, the owner said, "Let me call my partner. I'll get right back to you." Within 24 hours, I was face-to-face with the owner, and we put together a deal for $3,350,000.

The deal was mine to lose, but I had to act quickly, as the owner was also pursuing a refinance as a backup plan. The real estate broker had an in-house mortgage officer who quickly got me a term sheet for a 75 percent loan-to-value mortgage. I put my feelers out for a local manager and found a great company with solid systems in place. The manager even expressed interest in buying a small share of the property with us. We quickly finished our financial analysis of the deal and created a summary of the project, which, in the syndication world, is called an offering memorandum. We sent out an email blast to all our existing investors, telling them about the property, and set up several webinars to pitch the deal. We had a great turnout, and in about forty-five days, we had our equity commitment in place. Forty percent of the investors in the deal were new contacts, while the rest were repeat investors with us in some capacity. I attribute our success in raising the funds so quickly to staying in regular contact with our current and prospective investors via our monthly newsletter. People tend to forget about you unless you stay in regular contact.

We had several twists and turns, and a few times we weren't sure whether we would close, but we got to the table a few weeks before the owner's mortgage expired. Because of the vacancies and the costs of improving the management of the complex, it took a while to become profitable. We also were not told that verbal permission had supposedly been given to several tenants to move out right after closing and use their security deposit as their last month's rent. A few other tenants moved out in the middle of the night with no notice at all. Within a month, 20 percent of the complex was vacant. We hadn't budgeted for that high of a turnover right out of the gate. We had committed to pay investors in the first quarter of ownership because this was an immediate cash-flowing deal with little value add needed. Unfortunately, we had to hold off on distributions for six months to handle the renovations. We are doing well now and are considering building more units and some self-storage on the site to further increase profits. If I had to do the deal over again, I would have been more conservative in my presentation to investors and shown more of a ramp-up period for profits. The lesson for you is to always under-promise and over-deliver when presenting deals to Cash Providers.

Joint Ventures

Syndications are to rental deals what joint ventures are to fix-and-flips. They are more complex versions of the same product, with a twist when it comes to how the Cash Provider is involved. They are typically used on larger transactions, like new construction deals and condo conversions. The Cash Provider is given a slice of the equity in the deal and can also get an interest rate on his or her money. These can be win-win arrangements for both parties and typically occur on larger, more complex deals involving higher investment amounts, higher risk, and higher profit potential.

Joint ventures are not always between a Cash Provider and a Deal Provider. In 2017, a basement remodeling company reached out to me. It had a large crew and completed more than 300 basement remodels a year. The owners were happy with their business but wanted to do some investing on the side and get involved with projects their team could work on when they were in between other jobs. We negotiated a joint venture arrangement in which my company would find the deal and the private money, and they would complete all renovations at cost and manage the whole renovation process. We agreed to split the profit fifty-fifty, which works out great. All I have to do is find deals and money, and they complete a top-quality renovation for us at their cost. It's a great example of what's possible with a joint venture.

Paper Investments

So far, this book has discussed real estate deals involving the purchase of a piece of property. There are other real estate investors who don't purchase the property; they purchase the paper. Investing in "paper" involves buying the debt on the property and becoming the bank or other party that is owed money from the property owner. The most common of these investments is buying mortgage debt and also investing in real estate tax liens. Both can be lucrative for many reasons. First, investors get some sort of interest due on the debt they purchase, which is their revenue stream. Second, if they are smart, they can purchase the debt at a discount on the value of the property, which protects their position. Third, most of these paper investments give the owner the right to foreclose on the property at some point in the future. If the investor purchases the debt for the right price, he or she can foreclose to take ownership at a deep discount. That said, we are not going to go into a deep discussion on paper investments in this book, as I haven't done much investing in that space. If you are interested in learning more about it, I highly recommend the book *Real Estate Note Investing* by Dave Van Horn. He makes the somewhat complicated subject of note investing simple and understandable for all levels of investors.

Before we move on, I should say that all the complex deals I outlined here should not be taken lightly. Although the profits can be attractive, the losses can be devastating. Don't be tempted by the dollars and jump into deals like these before you are ready. I highly recommend that all Deal Providers start small and work their way up in deal complexity. It's better to make your mistakes, course-correct, and learn the important lessons on the smaller deals than on ones you may not be able to recover from if they go south.

Risks to Consider

Many new investors get sucked into the lure of more complex deals because they tend to have bigger dollar signs attached to them. Deals like this can be tempting because of the high rewards they may seem to yield, but they also have more potential for failure and bring a much larger element of complexity to the table in exchange for the potential for higher profits. The biggest risk that you can take on with these deals is not properly considering the risks that they carry. Jumping into a complex project without taking the time you need to understand all the intricacies can be catastrophic. You need to take the time to research what goes into these projects before you find a deal. Find the ways that you could lose, and work your way around them. Getting your head around the legal requirements, entity structure, government regulations, management structure, financing, and other factors is required before you even start looking for this type of project.

Keys to Success

As we wrap up this chapter on the Deal Provider, I want to give you three keys to success. If you follow these, you will build over time a following of committed investors and people who source you the best deals.

KEY NO. 1 | Under-Promise and Over-Deliver

This phrase gets thrown around a lot, so let's break it down a bit. *Under-promise* means not overselling yourself or overcommitting—ever. If you say you are going to do something, do it, or have a solid unexpected circumstance that prevented you from honoring your word. If you project returns on a deal and don't meet them, have a solid explanation for your investors of why you didn't hit your return threshold. Don't overhype your deals or put out the absolute best-case scenario as your projection either. It may feel good to put those pie-in-the-sky numbers out there, and it may generate more investors for you on your first deal, but you will quickly be discovered as someone who over-promotes projects and can't hit targets. The second part of that phrase— *over-deliver*—is all about your keeping your eye on the ball while your deal is in progress to make sure you hit your target. In a nutshell, set achievable, realistic goals—and then work your tail off to exceed them.

KEY NO. 2 | Communication Is Everything

You never want people scratching their heads, wondering what's going on, especially when you have their money. Keep people in the loop, during good times and bad—especially the bad because no one likes a surprise or wants to find out that you've been hiding something unpleasant. People don't expect these deals to go perfectly, and if you have their investment, they most likely trust you will figure it out. We provide ongoing updates via email newsletters as well as YouTube videos to keep our investors up-to-date, and it's a good way to show them the project they are invested in firsthand.

In my experience, I have found that most people under-communicate. People are moving so fast and are so busy that they don't take the time to keep people in the loop and informed. Remember, not everyone communicates as you do. You need to adapt your communication style to meet the needs of others, especially your Cash Providers. It is best to establish regular, ongoing communication strategies to keep your investors updated. Use a mix of communication strategies, such as email, video, project management apps (such as Slack), and the good old method of picking up the phone and calling.

KEY NO. 3 ▮ Fall in Love with This Business

There will be many days when the real estate investment business may be hard to love, but for the most part, you should find real joy in real estate investing or at least parts of it. If you don't like what you do, people will see it. Your Cash Providers will want to see your passion for what you do, and passion is contagious. If you are excited, they will be, too, and will most likely tell others about how you helped them grow over time. Your love for the business will also help you get through the not-so-fun parts, so be sure to remember what you love about investing so that you can remind yourself when the going gets tough.

CHAPTER 4
THE CASH PROVIDER

Russell Conwell, founder and first president of Temple University, gave a very inspirational speech in the early 1900s called "Acres of Diamonds," which was then turned into a book he authored of the same name. I am going to paraphrase his lecture as we jump into the topic of Cash Providers.

Not far from the River Indus, there once lived a Persian farmer by the name of Ali Hafed, who owned a large farm with orchards and gardens. He was a very wealthy man. One day he was visited by a traveling merchant from the East. The man told Ali Hafed how vast, rich veins of diamonds were being discovered all around the continent. Ali dreamed of how he could be even wealthier if only he had diamonds.

The next day Ali sold his farm and went off to search for diamonds. He searched all across the land. He went to the Middle East and found none. He went to Europe and found none. When the last of his money had been spent, he stood in rags at Spain's Bay of Barcelona, watching the waves roll in. Soon the penniless man cast himself into the oncoming tide and sank beneath the water, never to rise again.

One day the man who purchased Ali Hafed's farm led his camel into the garden to drink. As the camel lapped the brook's clear water, the man noticed a curious flash in the shallow stream's white sands. Reaching into the water, he withdrew a black pebble with an eye of light that reflected all the colors of the rainbow. He took the curious stone into the house, put it on the mantel, and returned to his chores.

Some days later, he was visited by the traveling merchant. The moment the merchant saw the gleam from the mantel, he rushed to it. "There's a diamond here!" he shouted. "A diamond! Has Ali returned?"

"No, he hasn't returned, and that's no diamond," the new owner answered. "I know a diamond when I see one," the merchant insisted. Together they rushed to the garden stream. They stirred the white sands with their fingers and, lo, discovered more stones, even more beautiful and valuable than the first. Thus, the diamond mine of Golconda was discovered, the most significant in history.

For decades, every shovelful from near that stream revealed gems that would decorate the crowns of monarchs. Had Ali Hafed remained at home and dug in his own garden instead of wandering aimlessly into a life of poverty, he would have had acres of diamonds.

One powerful takeaway of Conwell's "Acres of Diamonds" lecture is that there are opportunities and wealth (i.e., Cash Providers) right in your own backyard. And you don't need to be born into a certain type of family, have a country club membership, or go to a certain school to get connected to people with money to invest with you. Take a look around—you are already standing on your own acres of diamonds.

As I said previously, the Cash Provider is the investor or lender of the private capital for the project. *The Deal Provider is the legs; the Cash Provider is the money.* Both are necessary in a transaction, and they both have their roles. And just as there are good Deal Providers and bad ones, there are also good and bad Cash Providers in this business.

What Makes a Cash Provider a Good Fit?

Cash Providers who are a good fit understand that their role is to properly vet out you and the deals you bring them, make a decision, and then trust that you will make the right call on their behalf. They will produce the funds for the project when they say they will, and they won't get cold feet and back out on you at the last second after they have made a decision to go with your deal. They will want regular updates on how you are doing with their investment but will not want to meddle in the day-to-day activities. They believe in you and trust you. They also understand that they can't do what you do, either because of time constraints or because of a certain skill set or expertise you possess. They are patient and willing to work with you on timing, and as long as you are able to deliver on your word, they will continue to work with you over and over. They will also refer you to others if you keep them happy. At the core, good Cash Providers probably like what they do for a living and want to keep doing it and are investing with you to diversify their wealth. They want truly hands-off, passive income, working with someone they can trust.

One of our Cash Providers is a dentist whom I became friends with when we both lived in Philadelphia while he was in dental school. He bought a practice soon after graduation and spends all his time either in his business or with his family. He has been an investor with me on almost all my deals—not with enormous checks, but each time, I know I can count on him to jump in with me on whatever I'm putting together. He's not getting in just because we are friends; he's investing because he trusts me to do the right thing. If he has a question, he calls, but he knows and respects both of our roles.

On the other hand, Cash Providers who are a bad fit don't see the real difference between you and them. They may try to devalue the role of the Deal Provider in their negotiations or make comments that what you are doing is not that complicated and that they could do it themselves if they wanted to. Be cautious of any Cash Providers who ask for a high level of control of the deal or those who have unrealistic expectations of your performance or requirements for updates. All these are signs that they don't trust you, and this lack of trust will come up over and over again in your relationship with them and can cause problems in the future. Unlike a Cash Provider who is a good fit, a bad fit will eventually want to invest full-time and become a Deal Provider. This is a problem for you because the provider will constantly be looking for ways to invest without your partnership in the near future.

I had a prospective private lender look at a flip with me. He wanted to come see the property before we closed, which was fine. He also asked to see my projected renovation costs and projected sales price, each of which is part of a normal discussion with a private lender. During the site tour, he kept pointing out areas that didn't need to be renovated, challenging my scope of work. He told me the roof was in good condition and didn't need to be changed. He made comments such as "Let the new buyer worry about that." He also kept bringing up how much money I was going to make on the project and said that he wished he had more time because he would do the project himself. We ended up agreeing that we couldn't see eye to eye on that deal. He is still in my investor database, but we have yet to do a project, and I don't think we ever will. Although I explained it multiple times to him, I don't believe he wanted to understand (or wanted to accept) our roles—he was not my business partner; he was a lender or equity provider on a deal. Remember: Be cautious of any potential Cash Provider who does not support the fact that *you* are the one in the driver's seat on the project.

Why Do They Need You?

It's tough to build wealth in today's world. Many years ago, investors who made healthy contributions through their retirement accounts into Wall Street–based stocks, paid down their houses over the long term, and saved up some extra cash for a rainy day would be able to retire wealthy. That's not the case anymore. It's not that Wall Street can't make you rich—it can and has for many people. However, for the passive investor, it's no longer a predictable vehicle for investments. It does have a place in financial planning, but most have realized that it can't be the only source of long-term wealth-building investment opportunities. People are learning that they need to look elsewhere. Just look at the number of crowdfunding sites popping up and direct sites that allow Cash Providers to give loans directly to business owners. There is a need for alternatives. To be successful in achieving their long-term wealth goals, investors need alternatives. They need Deal Providers like yourself, who have integrity and whom they can trust. It's important to remember that they need us as much as we need them, especially when you start presenting your deals to potential Cash Providers.

To understand Cash Providers, you need to understand the source of their cash, meaning where their money is coming from. Knowing where your Cash Providers' capital is coming from will allow you to better understand their goals and what deals work best for them. It will also give you some clues to watch for when you start looking in your network for your first round of Cash Providers.

CASH SOURCE PART I ▍ The Self-Directed IRA

Self-directed individual retirement accounts (SDIRAs) are perhaps the most misunderstood and underused investment vehicle for new investors. That said, they are my favorite source of capital for deals. In essence, an SDIRA is a retirement account owned and controlled by a person, not a company or a mutual fund. Instead of being controlled by a third-party account manager, it is controlled by the account holder, who is the person who will receive the funds when upon retirement. The money is held by a third party (called a custodian), but the direction of investment is made by the account holder.

These IRAs can invest in all sorts of things. Of course, they can buy mutual funds just like other retirement accounts. In addition, they can also buy stocks and bonds directly, invest in partnerships, buy precious metals, buy real estate, and even lend money. There are very few restrictions on SDIRAs regarding what they can invest in. They are very restricted on who can make money from the activities of the IRA. There are certain people who cannot benefit in any way from the IRA's activities. These people are called disqualified persons. They can't own a piece of the investment alongside the IRA, be the borrower of the funds, take a fee from the transaction, or in any way make money or otherwise benefit from the IRA's activities.

Disqualified Person No. 1 – This one is perhaps the most obvious, and that is the account holder. It perhaps goes without saying that you can't invest your retirement account money and benefit personally from it in some way. Account holders get the long-term benefit of having their retirement account at work in a real estate project, which is a benefit they will realize when they start drawing on that account at retirement age. They can't take personal benefit from the activities of the IRA before then, though.

Disqualified Person No. 2 – The lineal ascendants of the account holder. In plain English, that means the parents, grandparents, great-grandparents, etc. (all the way up the family tree in a linear line). Their spouses are included in that exclusion, as well, so if your father is remarried, you can't lend the money to his wife.

Disqualified Persons No. 3 – The lineal descendants of the account holder. You can probably guess this means going the other way down the family tree to include the account holder's children, grandchildren, etc. (and, again, their spouses).

We could get into a deep discussion here on why these rules exist, but it's better to just say that these are the rules and the IRS enforces them. They will gladly fine the IRA holder a 10 percent penalty and charge income tax as if the person had withdrawn the funds from his or her retirement account. It's better to just play by the rules and invest your IRA funds somewhere else, if you have them.

Rules That Make SDIRAs Fantastic

There are two rules that regulate SDIRAs and make them incredible investment sources. One of these rules benefits the Deal Provider, and the other helps the Cash Provider.

RULE NO. 1 I *Account holder can't touch the money.*

As we already went over, the account holder cannot benefit personally from the SDIRA's activities in any way. Let's say you borrow money from a Cash Provider's SDIRA for a six-month fix-and-flip project. The Cash Provider doesn't benefit from monthly payments as he would have if he had lent the money out of his own pocket. The provider can't touch those payments anyway. The gain to the SDIRA is the same if the interest payments are paid monthly versus their being paid at the end of the loan period. This is extremely beneficial to the Deal Provider, who can preserve his cash and put it into the deal versus having to set aside cash for monthly payments.

RULE NO. 2 I *Income tax is not paid annually.*

One of the main benefits of retirement accounts is that the account holders do not have to pay tax on the profit they make each year. As with most other retirement accounts, the account holders pay tax on their account when they take the money out at retirement or before they put it in (as with a Roth SDIRA). Either way, they can take all the profit they make and roll it into the next project. If an account holder has $100,000 on January 1, invests in a private loan with a Deal Provider at 10 percent interest, and is paid back on December 31 of that year, the holder has $110,000 available for the next project and doesn't have to set aside any of that money to pay Uncle Sam. If you extrapolate that scenario out, the interest you pay to Cash Providers becomes fuel for exponential growth of their IRA. This is a *huge* advantage for Cash Providers and a big incentive for the provider to use an IRA when issuing private loan investments.

What I described above is called compounded interest. It's the action of taking the interest you earn on an investment and rolling it back into that investment, also known as earning interest on your interest. Compounded interest will grow an investment exponentially and even more so when the investor is not paying tax each time he or she takes an interest payment.

Einstein discovered a rule around compounding interest, called the Rule of 72.

The Rule of 72 goes like this: *If you take an investment that is compounded annually and divide the interest rate into the number 72, the result you will get is the number of years it will take that money to* double.

For example, let's say you have a Cash Provider, Sue. She lends $100,000 out of her SDIRA to a Deal Provider (Dave) for a fix-and-flip project at 10 per-cent interest. The project takes exactly one year to complete, at which point Dave gives Sue back $110,000. Dave has another deal lined up right behind this one, and they carry on like this, doing a deal a year. Seventy-two divided by the interest rate of 10 percent equals 7.2 years. Assume that Sue is thirty years old and doesn't invest in her SDIRA any further, but she continues to work with Dave as a lender on his fix-and-flips.

At thirty-seven years old, Sue has $200,000.

At forty-four years old, Sue has $400,000.

At fifty-one years old, Sue has $800,000.

At fifty-eight years old, Sue has $1,600,000.

And at the retirement age of sixty-five, *Sue has $3,200,000!*

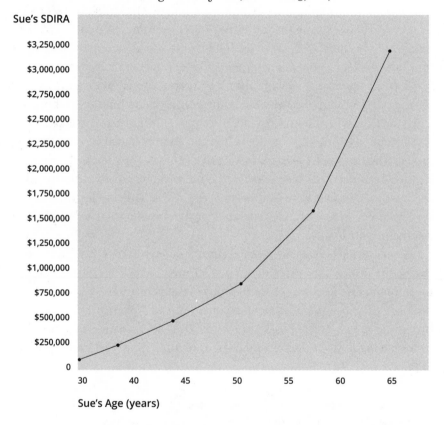

Not bad for an initial investment of $100,000. Remember, she didn't put any more money into her SDIRA; she only took what Dave paid her and rolled it into the next deal.

Rule No. 2 for SDIRAs is truly magic, but most people with IRAs don't know about it. There is a huge opportunity for Deal Providers to get out there and show this to those in their network who have these types of accounts.

The Facts That Help You Find the Money

All of this leads to the question, "How do you find these IRA holders?" They are really all around you; you just need to know where to look and how IRAs work. If you remember these facts about IRAs, you will have some clues about how to find them in your own network.

FACT NO. 1 | *What an IRA is and isn't.*

First, remember that an IRA is a retirement account for an *individual.* These accounts can be owned by the self-employed, anyone who either owns one company or is a sole proprietor. It's not a 401(k), which is a retirement account set up by a company for its employees. These accounts are much more prevalent than IRAs, but 401(k)s cannot be used in real estate transactions as IRAs can. That said, as soon as an employee leaves a company, that 401(k) retirement account *becomes* an IRA. This happens when the employee retires or leaves the job for any reason.

FACT NO. 2 | *Time and good companies help retirement accounts grow.*

You should know that although compounded interest applies to real estate loans, it applies to all retirement accounts. The stock market and mutual funds sometimes yield positive returns, and when they do, those returns are rolled back into the investment to create more growth. Additionally, good companies pay something called a company match to their employees in the form of an additional contribution to an employee's retirement account on top of what the employee puts in on his or her own. Not all companies do this, but the larger ones do. If you factor in compounded interest and a company match, you see that the longer the employee works at the company, the larger his or her 401(k) account is likely to be.

FACT NO. 3 | *An IRA is not a self-directed IRA.*

Just because you find someone with an IRA doesn't mean that you can immediately start doing deals with them. Regular IRAs that are managed by financial planners or retirement specialists cannot be used to invest in real estate. Don't be surprised if your Cash Provider's financial planner tries to talk him or her out of doing this type of investing or even says it's not possible because it's not through accounts that are managed by him or her. The financial planner is the director of the retirement account. He or she places the investments on behalf of the account owner. A self-directed IRA is controlled by the account holder directly; the financial planner is out of the picture. To work with you, the Cash Provider needs to roll his or her existing IRA over to an SDIRA company, of which there are plenty to choose from.

Considering all the above, there are a few clues to look for when searching your network for good IRA Cash Providers. Try looking for people who *used to* have a good job with a good company that provided lots of benefits, like company-paid health care and a company match to their 401(k) account. They worked at that company for a reasonable amount of time, probably more than seven years for the retirement account to have something substantial in it. They have since moved on to another job, so that 401(k) can be rolled over to an SDIRA and invested with you.

The Perfect Deals for SDIRAs

Let's review the greatest benefits of an SDIRA so that we can get clear on how a Deal Provider can best leverage those benefits to create the best opportunities for the potential Cash Providers. The first benefit is that an SDIRA is tax deferred. As I already covered, SDIRAs don't pay tax annually; they pay it when the money is actually taken out of the account. If they are invested in a deal with a large return that would normally be taxed at ordinary rates, they are not subject to that tax. To take full advantage of this benefit, you should invest these accounts in things that have no built-in tax advantages and are normally taxed heavily. The second benefit is that SDIRAs can participate in the magic of compounded interest. To do that, they need to get their money and interest back in a reasonable period of time so that you can roll it back into a deal. This return of capital should happen at least once a year to abide by the Rule of 72.

Considering these benefits, two investment vehicles are ideal for SDIRAs.

VEHICLE NO. 1 | Short-Term Private Loans
Interest on private loans does not have any benefits from a tax perspective; it is taxed as ordinary income. If the loan is used on a fix-and-flip or BRRRR (buy, rehab, rent, refinance, repeat, as a reminder) property, the loan term should be much less than one year. I have found that this vehicle is by far the easiest and best way to get started with a new Cash Provider. These deals are almost always less than a year and have lots of collateral, so the investment

is safe and the return is predictable. Even smaller SDIRAs in the $25,000 to $50,000 range can be used on deals if the structure is done properly.

VEHICLE NO. 2 | Fix-and-Flips

Flips have a short time horizon, typically less than a year. Additionally, fix-and-flip projects are taxed as short-term capital gains, which is avoided when using an SDIRA. To take full advantage, the Cash Provider needs to be at least part owner of the flipped property and participate in the profits of the sale. Not every Deal Provider is willing to give away some ownership to the Cash Provider on these deals, but if the deal and the prospective investment are large enough, you may be able to find some room for the provider.

Final Thoughts on SDIRAs

Most people over thirty who have worked at more than one job in their career have some sort of retirement account that can be converted into an SDIRA. They are most likely all around you. These accounts have incredible benefits to both the Cash Provider and the Deal Provider and, when used properly, will help both parties build their wealth. As a Deal Provider, it pays to know how to best benefit the Cash Provider's IRA to give him or her the highest growth potential. The Deal Providers who are able to provide these vehicles and explain them clearly to their Cash Providers will have plenty of money at their fingertips for all their projects.

CASH SOURCE PART II | Real Estate Equity

One of the biggest jobs of good Deal Providers is educating their investors on what is possible with the investor's assets. Many Cash Providers have no idea that they have potential investment capital at their fingertips. The IRA holders discussed in the section above may or may not have any idea what they can do with their retirement account, but at least they know that they have investable capital.

In my eyes, the biggest area of potential investment capital that Cash Providers don't even realize they have is real estate equity. Many Deal Providers may be able to free up some cash to do their own deals if they know where to look. In this case, the real estate equity I am referring to is the difference in the market value of a home and what the homeowner's current mortgage balance is. If the mortgage balance is less than 50 percent of the home's value, there is potential to unlock some of that equity.

There may not even be a mortgage. At the time I'm writing this, around 30 percent of homeowners in the United States own their houses free and clear, without any mortgage at all. When I first heard this, it blew me away. While many Americans refinanced their houses to the max during the housing bubble, many just kept paying their monthly payments like clockwork until their house was paid off. There are also techniques that have become popular out there to pay down a thirty-year fixed mortgage in under twenty years. Either through discipline or otherwise, many Americans have no mortgage or monthly debt payment on their home.

Others own other property free and clear. I have investors who work with me through equity in their vacation homes and another investor whose primary business is a hotel. They were able to unlock additional equity in those assets and put it to work in passive investments with my company. When you start looking for it, you will see that real estate equity is *everywhere*, waiting to get unlocked and put to work.

How to Unlock the Equity

Aside from just selling the property and taking the proceeds, the only way to tap into real estate equity is to borrow against it. There are a few methods you can use, depending on the Cash Providers' goals for investments and their risk tolerance.

METHOD NO. 1 | *New Mortgage*

The owner of the property can simply refinance it with a new mortgage or get a second mortgage to pull out what cash he or she can. Almost any bank that does residential loans will be willing to accommodate this, as long as the homeowner has good credit and a steady source of income. This is most likely the simplest and most obvious option, but there are some things to consider.

The first consideration is that the owners of a property will immediately have to start making monthly payments on the debt, even if they don't have any cash flow yet from their investments. This needs to be considered, as owners will have to "carry" this debt on their own until they have somewhere to invest the cash for a return. Owners need to be prepared for this, as they will want to take their time to shop deals until they find something that works for their goals. The worst types of investments to make are ones that you make with a sense of urgency that could have been avoided by being prepared.

The second consideration is that the interest rate is most likely fixed on this mortgage, meaning the payment won't go up or down through the life of the loan. This is a major benefit to Cash Providers, as it gives them a fixed and predictable cost of their capital. As long as their investment yields a return that's higher than the monthly payment on the debt, they are making cash flow. What's great about this is that Cash Providers can create a stream of income for themselves without going into their personal cash to create it. It's even better if the payments are amortized (meaning a portion goes toward paying the mortgage balance off).

Another consideration is access to the cash. If your Cash Provider has not begun the process of refinancing his or her real estate, it can take upward of sixty days for the provider's cash to become available for investment in your deal. Great deals may not stick around for sixty days, waiting for the money to come in, so this cash source is best used for deals that have a longer timeline. It won't work for those "need to close next week" types of projects.

When you look at a mortgage and see the factors I listed above (fixed rate, fixed monthly payments), it makes sense that these types of loans work well on long-term rental deals. Your Cash Providers can also lend or invest in fix-and-flips with you, but remember they will have to keep carrying those monthly payments while you are searching for the next deal. Rentals provide monthly revenue checks when they are stable, which can then pay the mortgage installments for your Cash Provider. Because the rates are fixed, you can help them predict their cash flow easily as long as you have rental revenue numbers you can stand behind.

Let's say that your uncle Harry decides to invest with you and his home is almost paid off. He decides to refinance his house with a fixed-rate mortgage on a fifteen-year amortization and is able to pull out $200,000 in cash after all loan fees are paid. If he borrows the money at 4 percent interest, his monthly payments are $1,479 per month. If he invests with you on a long-term hold rental deal through which he makes a 12 percent cash-on-cash return on his money, his revenue is $24,000 per year. Take the cost of capital at $1,499 and multiply by 12 to get $17,748. That's a net cash flow to Uncle Harry of just over $6,000 per year. But it gets better. If you and Uncle Harry agree to hold the rental for 15 years, at the end of it, that rental has paid his mortgage 100 percent off, and he still has his share of the rental property he bought with you—and cash flow for fifteen years on top.

METHOD NO. 2 | *Home Equity Line of Credit*
A HELOC is very similar to a mortgage but with a very important twist. The equity line gives borrowers the right to borrow against the equity in their

home but doesn't give them a lump sum of cash as a refinance does. If they don't borrow against the line, they have no monthly payments. When they do borrow, the payments are associated only with what they have out on the line of credit. Although it's called a *home* equity line of credit, Cash Providers can tap into equity they have in a second home, a rental property, or a business real estate that they own. It's a very flexible source of capital, but just as with a mortgage, there are a few factors to consider.

In a mortgage, the rate is typically fixed and the loan is amortized down over time. In a HELOC, the rate most likely changes on a monthly basis and the payments are interest only. This is great short term, as the cost of capital is very low for borrowed money. That being said, HELOCs are subject to rate fluctuations over time, which can hurt a long-term hold deal that is dependent on a specific monthly payment for the debt.

In my experience, a HELOC is best for investors who want to be nimble and able to get in and out of short-term deals. If there is not a deal in the works, they don't have any unnecessary monthly expenses to carry their cash waiting to be invested. Once they are in a deal, the carrying costs of that debt are low, and once the deal is complete, they can pay back their HELOC and wait for the next deal to come around.

METHOD NO. 3 | *Business Equity Lines*
This type of loan is a derivation of a HELOC with another important twist. Let's say that you are looking to get some additional capital to grow your real estate business and you go to a bank looking for a business loan. You don't own much property with equity, as you are just getting started, but you have good credit. Your uncle Harry, who owns his home free and clear, believes in you and is willing to help you out. He is interested in working with you but doesn't want to deal with managing the money coming in and out of the accounts; he just wants to put his real estate equity in your control. The bank can issue a business equity line of credit (BELOC) to your company, with Uncle Harry as a guarantor on the BELOC and his home as collateral. You become the borrower and the controller of the funds and are responsible for the monthly payments. Uncle Harry's house is the collateral for the loan, which means if the Deal Provider is not responsible with the money and is not able to keep up with the payments, the bank can come and take Uncle Harry's real estate.

These loans operate just as HELOCs do, with floating rates and interest-only payments. This is a great vehicle to get you started, but as you can imagine, it takes an immense amount of trust between you and the guarantor who is backing this loan for you. The Deal and Cash Providers need to figure out a way to compensate the Cash Provider for being the guarantor, which is where understanding the goals of each party and finding a win-win comes in. Perhaps the Cash Provider gets a small slice of each fix-and-flip deal that gets completed. This type of arrangement is not for everyone, as it takes high trust on the Cash Provider's side and a high level of financial responsibility on the Deal Provider's.

Deals That Work Best for HELOCs (and BELOCs)

These types of loans are best for projects that have a clear beginning, middle, and end. You don't want something with a floating rate as a long-term source of capital, because that rate can change and turn your deal upside down. Once these loans are in place and ready for a deal, they work very well for purchases that need a quick closing because the cash can be accessed very quickly, normally within twenty-four to forty-eight hours. These loans also work well for deals that need lots of construction because the money can be borrowed as it's needed, and the borrower pays interest only on what is outstanding at the time.

For all these reasons, HELOCs and BELOCs work best for fix-and-flip projects and for the BRRRR strategy for investments. Most of the time, fix-and-flips and BRRRR deals involve distressed real estate. You're most likely going to see deals like this at auctions, estate sales, bank-owned sales, and places where an offer with a quick cash closing is going to get the deal. Having one of these cash sources lined up will allow you to make "cash" offers with the confidence that you can close in a few weeks if needed. You will also be able to complete renovations quickly and with low carrying costs. As long as you have your exit strategy planned out properly, you can be very successful with flips and BRRRR projects using HELOCs and BELOCs.

A Tale of Caution: Begin with the End in Mind

When Liz and I first got started, we were able get two BELOC loans in place, one on my parents' primary residence and another on my wife's parents' vacation home. These two lines of credit opened up access to large amounts of cash to us, just over $500,000. This was in 2006, so the market was on a nice run-up, and it was making everyone who was investing in real estate look really smart. We bought rentals, repaired them, and refinanced them to get the line of credit money back. This was going well, so we scaled up.

We started buying rentals with bank financing and used the lines of credit as equity on the purchase. This worked fine in an up market, as we could eventually refinance the property to pull out the line of credit. When the market crashed in 2008, we ended up having to hold some rentals with the lines of credit tied up in them. We never missed a payment on the loans, but having to make a first mortgage payment and a line of credit payment really put a damper on our cash flow. The market took a while to recover, so we were stuck with some break-even rentals. Had we kept playing the short game with the lines of credit, we would have never used them to provide the equity on a long-term hold. In hindsight, all I needed was a mentor who could have guided us on using these lines of credit to our benefit. Lines of credit can be incredible vehicles for growth, but they can also be weapons of mass destruction if used improperly.

Finding Real Estate Equity Sources in Your Network

The good thing about these sources of equity is that they are everywhere. The bad thing is that they are everywhere! Unfortunately, a free-and-clear house looks just like a house with a mortgage on it. Here are some clues to look for when searching in your personal network:

- Any home that was bought between 2009 and 2011 has surely seen a rise in value, especially in areas where the real estate crash hit hard.
- Vacation homes are sometimes owned free and clear, financed by owners refinancing their primary residence to pay for the vacation home.
- Houses owned for more than fifteen years. As long as the owners didn't refinance in the real estate boom, the homes are most likely paid off or close to it.
- Businesses that own real estate but are not real estate investment companies. Look for small-business owners in your circle who own small office buildings, warehouses, hotels, or other real estate assets. To keep their expenses down, they may own these properties free and clear.

CASH SOURCE PART III | Cash

In the past two cash source discussions, Cash Providers may not even know that they have the cash or that they can put it to work in passive real estate investments. It's the job of the Deal Provider to educate them about that potential investment capital they have access to. That said, there is another group of investors who know they have money. These are investors who have cash. These investors may also have real estate assets or retirement accounts, which can be accessed, but cash investments should be viewed differently from other sources.

There are many ways that an investor can come across a large amount of cash. As you get to know them, see whether you can find out how they got the cash. Knowing this will help guide you to the best investment vehicles to recommend that will suit their goals and risk tolerance. Here are a few likely cash sources, how to look for them, and how to work with investors of these cash sources.

CASH SOURCE NO. 1 | Inheritance

At some point in life, many people will have a windfall inheritance left to them. This is usually a bittersweet occurrence because it takes the loss of someone close to them. They may be surprised with what is left to them, leaving them both grieving their loss but also not sure what to do with this new cash.

The last thing I suggest you do is start looking for funerals in your circles and asking, "Hey, did anyone get left any money, and if so, do they want to invest it in real estate?" You have to approach these things with tact, but odds are the money was unexpected, and when they are ready, the people who received the inheritance will be looking to do something with it. The question is, "How can they take this final gift from their loved one and better their lives or the lives of their families with it?" If they are willing to talk to you, get to know their financial goals. Do they need or could they use additional monthly cash flow? Maybe they have a three-year-old and want to create a college account for him or her. There are tax-deferred accounts they can put that cash in, then use the Rule of 72 discussed previously to double that money a few times before their child turns eighteen. There are many ways that you can work with them if you get clear on what their five- to ten-year plan is for their lives. As long as you approach them with respect and a genuine desire to help them, you can really help them make the most of this unexpected gift.

CASH SOURCE NO. 2 | Savings

Liz and I got married in 2005. Right after we got engaged, we started talking about combining finances once we were married, and we took a look at each other's bank accounts to see what we would be starting with. I fell out of my chair when I saw how much money my wife had saved up. I think she still had the money from her first Holy Communion gifts! Liz is a big-time saver.

If she doesn't need the money that month, it goes into a savings account, and she pretends it's not there.

There are many other well-disciplined savers out there. You might be surprised at how much some people have sitting in their savings accounts. The problem for these savers is that they are losing money because the rate they get paid on it doesn't even keep up with inflation. Saving significant amounts of money in a bank account is a losing game in the long run.

The problem that a Deal Provider has is that cash sources like this are hard to find. Savers don't buy flashy cars or live in big houses. They may not talk about investing out in the open either. They are very price conscious, even frugal with their money. That doesn't mean that everyone who is tight with their money is a big saver, but I have found that savers are almost always very price aware. Take it from someone who's married to one.

To invest with a saver, you have to understand him or her. Most savers I know hold their money with very high regard and are very conservative with it. High-risk deals (with little or no collateral, for instance) will not be for them. They will, however, love the concept of a nice, conservative private loan at a reasonable interest rate with lots of collateral. If your saver is very conservative, you could probably negotiate an interest rate that's very beneficial to you if you offer up more security, like a lower loan-to-value rate or even a personal guarantee along with a mortgage on the property.

CASH SOURCE NO. 3 | Savvy Investors

If you stay in this business long enough, you will meet "professional investors." They may have a background in finance or training in investments, or they may have learned the ropes hands on over the years. Wherever they learned it, they know (or they think they know) about passive investments and may have already done apartment building deals, private loans, or other vehicles as Cash Providers in the past.

They will typically show you who they are by the questions they ask. They will want to know what the internal rate of return is on your deal, whether you have researched the demographics around your most recent purchase, or whether you have a contingency reserve on the fix-and-flip you are doing. When you meet people like this, you'd better have your A game together. If your deal is not fully baked yet, tell them that and ask whether you can meet when you have all the data. Don't try to wing it; they will see right through that. If you are newer to the game, tell them. They may even be willing to help you. You should be direct with them and ask them to help you get a better understanding of the types of deals they like to do and what their investment criteria are and then go out and find a deal. If you show them one and they shoot it down, ask why so that you can better understand their goals. They may invest only with Deal Providers who have an established track record. If that's the case, keep in touch with them as you grow your business. You may need to start with other investors and then come back to them when you can show them some successful deals you've completed.

Investors like this will most likely tell you what kind of deals they like to do; they won't beat around the bush. If they like apartment buildings, they will tell you. If they want to do short-term private loans and play the Rule of 72, they will make that known also. Most savvy investors I have dealt with are open to most things, as long as they don't have some sort of aversion to what you are doing.

I have one investor I had been approaching for years trying to get him to work with me. He kept turning down deal after deal that I sent him, and finally I took him out to lunch. I asked him why he kept looking at my deals but wouldn't invest. He told me that he did fix-and-flips only when he got a small chunk of the profit and wouldn't do a rental deal unless there was an investor benefit called a preferred return, which is a minimum return on investment that gets paid to the Cash Provider first, before any profit gets paid out to the Deal Provider. I had not done a deal that involved a preferred return to this point, but I let him tell me all about the other ones he had done and how they worked out. He educated me on how to set these deals up. A year or so later, an apartment building deal came up that worked well to offer a preferred return. He was one of my first calls, and he gladly jumped into the deal with me.

CASH SOURCE NO. 4 | High-Income Earners

Most of you probably figure that people who earn a lot of money have a lot of money. This can be true, but it's not always the case. They could be living paycheck to paycheck; they just have more expenses to absorb all that income they have. There are other high-income earners who live below their means and have money to put to work but not the time to manage it.

Some of my best investors are people who went through years of training to do what they do for a living and get paid well for doing it. Dentists and doctors are good examples of this. They went to school for more than ten years, in some cases, to get to their position. They are not going to leave that job anytime soon, but they get paid very well for doing what they do and are often looking for opportunities to grow their wealth.

If you have a solid relationship with someone like this, he or she may even be willing to act as a sponsor for you on a loan. A sponsor is someone who has good income and assets and steps in as an additional guarantor on a loan. This is of value for those of you who are just getting started with little or no track record. It will also help if you are in this business full-time, as banks like to see earned income from a job or a well-established business from their guarantors. The presence of a sponsor becomes even more important on larger deals, which don't require a personal guarantee, but the bank will still want to see a large amount of assets sitting behind the owner that can be used if the deal gets into trouble.

Success Leaves Clues

Whether they hit the lottery or came across a large pot of money by complete mistake, there is probably an interesting story and a lesson behind how people got their money. Even in the case of an inheritance, the person who left that inheritance must have done something right to amass enough money to leave a life-changing sum to his or her descendants. Find out their story. How did that savvy investor get started? Did they get training on passive investments in school or figure it out themselves, or did someone teach it to them? What are the habits that saver implements in his life that enabled him to set aside that much cash for his family? What are his spending habits? What did that person's father or mother do to create that much wealth to leave as a legacy for his or her children?

You want to know these stories, not just to get to know and understand your potential Cash Providers better but to hear the stories of their success. Most of the time, success is not an accident. It is the product of an applied formula, time, mind-set, and sometimes a little bit of luck. Find out what their formula was. You will surely get some life lessons and inspiration to create some of these habits yourself. Approach people with the desire to learn the story of their wealth. Let your pitch to invest with you be something that naturally comes up after you've heard their story. Getting to know their story will also help you think like them so that you can find more of these cash sources in your circles. As you grow your business, you will learn how to tailor certain projects for your cash source investors and other projects for the investors you have from other sources.

TAX | *The Biggest Factor with Cash Investments*

With SDIRAs, the returns are tax deferred, meaning investors don't have to pay tax on their returns until they take the money out. Cash investors can't hide; they have to pay tax each year on what they earn from their investments. This brings up two factors that you need to make sure your Cash Providers understand before getting into a deal with you. One can hurt them, while the other is a huge benefit.

Capital Gains Tax

Each year we all file our taxes with the IRS, telling it how much we made for the year, which calculates what we owe in taxes. As you probably know, your income is broken down into several buckets. Your primary job is the first bucket, called your earned or ordinary income. This is money you make every year and will continue to do so as long as you keep your job. Other buckets include passive income from hands-off investments, dividends on businesses you own, interest received on your money in a savings account or lent to other people, and capital gains. Capital gains are looked at by the IRS as one-time events, most likely not repeated every year. There are short-term gains, which you realize from activity that took less than a year, and long-term gains from activity that took more than a year to come to fruition. A fix-and-flip project will most likely take less than a year from beginning to end, so those profits will probably be short-term gains.

The IRS taxes short-term capital gains and interest income the same way—as ordinary income. That means that if a Cash Provider invests in a fix-and-flip with you as a lender or owner, and the project takes less than a year to complete, the provider pays the same tax rate as he or she pays on the money earned at his or her job. Long-term capital gains tax is less, between 15 and 20 percent these days, but that means that it took over a year to finish the deal, which is most likely not in the Deal Provider's best interest regarding business momentum!

If your Cash Providers are in a high tax bracket, they will have to pay a large amount of money on their flip and interest revenue with you, which will diminish their returns. Even if they are not high-income earners, they still need to be aware of how these investments are taxed so that they know to set aside a portion of their income with you for their tax obligations. You should advise them to speak with their CPA on the investment they are making with you.

In my business, my CPA is invaluable. I speak to him regularly about the tax obligations on my deals and also about how what I'm doing will affect the Cash Providers working with me. I would encourage you to make sure that your CPA really knows real estate well. There are a lot of moving parts when it comes to taxes, and your CPA will be able to help you the best. One of the things we love most about our CPA is that he is a real estate investor as well. This has helped tremendously as we have grown and expanded our investing business.

Depreciation

Although the IRS does not look favorably on income from fix-and-flips, income from rental properties is very favorably viewed. Let's start off by talking about how companies report their income.

Individuals make money, and then they pay tax on what they made, and then they pay their bills with what's left. Companies make money and pay their bills, and then what's left is taxable. This is a great benefit for companies, as business owners get to reduce their tax burden by taking on more expenses. What makes it even better with rentals is that the IRS allows us to claim an expense that we don't have to write a check for, called depreciation.

Depreciation is an allowance for the slow deterioration in value of an asset. Most things lose their value over time if they are not maintained, and the same is true for real estate. The IRS allows real estate owners to write off a portion of the value of their property each year as an expense against the property's income. The amount you get to write off each year has to do with what type of property it is (in my experience, residential property gets a better write-off than commercial). It also depends on how you handle the machinery and fixtures that have a shorter life than the building does, like the furnaces, light fixtures, and appliances.

A good CPA will show you how to maximize your depreciation benefits. What I want you to remember is that if the property cash flow is $10,000 at the end of the year and depreciation was $6,000, the taxable income for you and your investors is $4,000. *But you actually made $10,000.* You didn't have to write that check for $6,000 to anyone; you just get to deduct it from the property's income.

I've even had investments in which my Cash Providers made a nice income from their rentals we owned that year, and they got to claim a *loss* on their tax return! It doesn't get any better than that. Depreciation is a huge benefit to Cash Providers who own rentals with you. The savvy investors probably already know about this and will be more intrigued by rental deals for that very reason. Other investors will need a little bit of education from the Deal Provider to see the long-term benefits.

Although depreciation has great advantages, there does come a time when you have to pay up, and that is when you sell the building. Assuming you sold the property for more than you paid for it, you will need to "recapture" the depreciation losses you took as part of your gain on the sale. However, you can do a 1031 exchange with your investors and roll that profit into another, larger deal. There is talk of removing the 1031 exchange from the tax code, but if it does get removed, I bet there will be something else put in its place that will have similar tax benefits.

Final Thoughts on Cash Providers

There are a few things I can't stress enough when working with Cash Providers. I would say to treat their money as if it's your own, but it's *not your money.* It's theirs. You need to be extremely respectful with how you invest it. You may be willing to take risks with your own cash, but always be more cautious with theirs. Your investors most likely view you as a vehicle to reach their long-term wealth goals. They are putting their financial future in your hands. This could be their kid's college money, their retirement money, or money they plan to leave to their children as a legacy one day. Don't ever take them or their money for granted. If your investors see the respect you hold for them and their investment, you will have lifelong partners who will get behind you again and again on your projects.

CHAPTER 5
WHERE TO FIND CASH PROVIDERS

I have talked to many budding real estate investors who want to get started in raising private capital but don't know where to find Cash Providers. This seems to be the biggest hurdle many Deal Providers experience. They find the deals but can't find the money to make it happen. This chapter will give you the road map for "finding the money," showing you where to start, when to take it to the next level, and what the next level will look like.

Introduction to the Cash Provider Pyramid

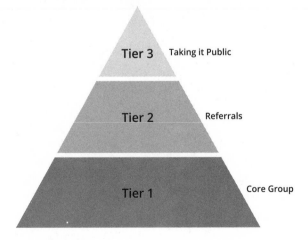

As I said earlier, many investors want to jump right in and put their first deal on a crowdfunding site. Perhaps they want to solicit an investor off the Internet for their first deal, which happens to be a one-hundred-unit apartment complex. All I can say is, "Slow down. You will get there if you put one foot in front of the other!"

I have found that there is a process to building up your private money resources, and I have illustrated it for you with the Cash Provider Pyramid. Using this method, you can get started right away with the people who already trust and respect you. As you expand, you can find a few people in your Tier 1 group who can become strategic partners to help you raise your contact base and deepen your Cash Provider database. When you hit your stride and have a decent track record, you can take your game to the highest level through social media and other public venues.

Let's start at the bottom and work our way up. I will break each tier down and give you the tools to maximize your efforts in each.

TIER 1 | Core Group

The first tier is your Core Group. These are people who already like, trust, and respect you. Most likely these are your friends and your family. These people don't need to see a track record from you; they are investing in *you* more than the deal.

As we jump into this topic, let's talk briefly about something that may be bugging some of you. It may make you uncomfortable thinking about pitching your uncles, aunts, old college roommates, or even your own parents about working with you in your real estate investing business. I understand. I went through the same thing when I started talking to my Core Group about what we were up to. What you need to remember is that these people are not investing as a favor to you. This is an opportunity for them. You can help them build their wealth. In today's investment world, *they need you*. Don't forget that. They are not sure what to do with their extra cash, their retirement accounts, or their other assets. They don't know what they don't know. It's up to you to educate them with confidence on how they can become a passive money partner in your business. You owe it to your close friends and family to tell them about what you are doing, not just to offer them an opportunity but also so that they can be excited for you. Even if they don't invest, if they believe in you, they will be your biggest cheerleaders.

When you first get started raising capital, you need to talk to *everyone* about what you do. When you go to a networking event, a neighborhood BBQ, or any other social function and people ask you what you do for a living, tell them you "invest in real estate." I promise you they won't change the subject. What we do as investors is interesting! You never know whom you will meet. You may strike up a conversation and hear someone say something like, "Boy, I sure wish I could invest in real estate, but I just don't have the time ..." Guess who does have the time to invest on his or her behalf? *You do.*

Another place to find prospective investors who already like and respect you are alumni groups from your high school or college. You never know—that person who sat next to you in history class may be working as a cardiologist with plenty of extra money and no time to invest. Social media sites like LinkedIn and Facebook are also great outlets to broadcast what you are up to. Be sure not to broadcast something like, "Hey, call me if you want to invest in real estate passively!" You don't want to do this for two reasons. One, it's tacky, and you probably won't get much traction. Two, it could be viewed as a solicitation, which is strictly prohibited by the SEC. You are better off posting something about how excited you are to be investing in real estate and what you are learning. If you are friends with any other real estate investors on Facebook, do you notice they put lots of cool pictures of their deals out all the time with nice updates on their progress? Some are doing this just because they love talking about their success on Facebook, but the smart ones are doing this to attract investors. If you have a fix-and-flip or rental deal in the works, put some updates online. You never know who will reach out to you.

I would also recommend you keep your eyes and ears open in *all* business, social, religious, and philanthropic organizations and clubs you are involved with. These include both the non–real estate investing groups as well as the real estate investing groups I mentioned in an earlier chapter. This can be the Rotary club, the chamber of commerce, the runner's club, and even a local meet-up for real estate investors. Please note that I am not suggesting you run up to these people and ask them to invest in your deals without establishing a relationship first. I will get into the "investor enrollment" process in a later chapter. However, I want you to begin considering people as potential Cash Providers whom you may not have before reading this book. Potential Cash Providers are all around you. You just need to begin seeing them.

Our First Private Money Deal

It just so happens that our very first private money deal involved an SDIRA lender, an equity investor, and the BRRRR strategy all wrapped into one deal. I was part of a BNI group years ago. We had a mixer one evening, and I started talking with one of the husbands of a member of the group. He wanted to buy a few rentals for himself, and he had an IRA lender lined up. I helped him with a few of his purchases and with his private lender funding all the purchase and construction costs. Seeing the benefits his lender was getting through his IRA, he wanted to do the same. He asked whether I could do the same arrangement with his retirement account, and I agreed. The equity investor was someone who went to college with my wife. They got reconnected on LinkedIn years after graduation and decided to get coffee to catch up. He was a very successful financial planner at the time, and during coffee he shared that he wanted to get into real estate but didn't have the time. My wife connected us, and we agreed to put together an equity partnership in which he would get 50 percent of the deal for putting his cash up and I would get 50 percent for arranging the purchase, construction, and management.

This was right after the real estate crash, so there were good deals all over. I put the word out to my local real estate agents and wholesalers who we were looking for a deal, giving them specifics on deal size and condition. It didn't take me long to find two townhomes for sale in Trenton, New Jersey, near my office. They were next to each other, selling for $22,000 each. Renovations would cost around $25,000, including new kitchens and baths, roofs, and flooring. Once renovated, they would lease for around $950 each. The lender with the IRA took a first-position mortgage for $25,000 on each house, $50,000 total, and agreed to take his interest when the properties were refinanced. My equity partner put up the other $50,000 through an LLC that he and I formed as fifty-fifty partners. The renovations came out great, and we were able to lease the houses out right away at my target of $950 per month. I then went to a local bank to refinance the properties to take out my private lender. The properties came in with a value of $50,000 each, which enabled us to take out the private lender and part of my equity investor's cash as well. The private lender was very happy and couldn't wait to do another deal with us. We had a chunk of equity in the company, as well, around $25,000 for the next deal.

Making Your Master List

Now that we have covered the sources of cash, I want you to take out a piece of paper and create your master core group list.

Step No. 1 – Write down the following headers:

- Friends
- Family
- Neighbors/neighborhood (this includes stores and restaurants you always go to)
- Coworkers
- College/graduate school alumni
- Groups and organizations you are a member of, such as:
  - Business networking organizations
  - Volunteer/philanthropic groups
  - Religious groups
  - Social groups
  - Real estate organizations

Step No. 2 – I want you to think about people in each of these groups who may fit the profile to be a Cash Provider for your business. Who would be a good source of IRA investment capital? Who may own their home free and clear? Who are the big savers in each of these circles? Start making a master list of all your contacts who fit the profile. Don't leave anyone out, even the people you aren't sure will be a good fit. Write down the names of the people you aren't comfortable approaching right now because as you grow, you can circle back to them.

Step No. 3 – For each column, write down the person's name, the suspected source of capital, and any pertinent notes you have on why they would be a good source. Go through *all* your contacts. Your family, classmates from the past, the owner of the restaurant you like to go to—everyone. You probably know more people than you think you do. You may want to try surfing your social media contacts to jog your memory.

To help you get your list going, I have summarized the cash sources here with a few signs to look for from each.

CASH SOURCE I *Retirement Accounts*
- People who used to have a high-paying job with a reputable company that most likely had a 401(k) program—even better if there was a company match. These people can't work for that company anymore.
- The self-employed, like doctors, attorneys, CPAs, and others who don't work for a big company but may have their own IRA program in-house
- Those who have retired from the workforce but worked for a good company in the past

CASH SOURCE I *Real Estate Equity*
- People who have lived in their house for more than fifteen years
- Homeowners who purchased between 2009 and 2011
- Anyone with a vacation home
- Businesses that own the buildings they occupy

CASH SOURCE I *Cash*
- Those who live well below their means
- High-income W-2 earners
- People who seem to already be investing in passive-income-producing assets
- Recent recipients of an inheritance

There are other things to look for; not everyone who has the above characteristics will end up being a viable Cash Provider to you. That said, making a master list will aid you in organizing the people in your network who will be members of your Tier 1 Core Group.

TIER 2 I Referrals

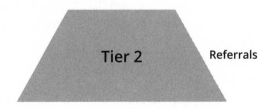

Remember that investor my wife went to college with? We now had two cash-flowing houses, a lender who wanted another deal, and $25,000 in the bank. My equity partner was happy, so he started telling his contacts about what we were up to. It didn't take long for one of his friends to offer to jump into another deal with us. I found a duplex and a single-family home for sale as a package for $90,000. A local wholesaler brought me the deal. The properties needed around $30,000 in work collectively. My equity partner's friend came up with $25,000, we put in our $25,000 left over from the refinance, and my private lender stepped in with a loan for $75,000. Once renovations were complete, we rented the units out, and refinanced to successfully take out the lender. There wasn't much equity left behind this time, but we did get the lender all the way out. Since that second deal, we've put together quite a few deals, and those two equity partners and my private lender have been a part of almost all of them.

I share this story to show how one thing can turn into another. People know other people, and if you take care of your Cash Providers, they will tell others of the good experiences they are having with you. When I look at my current list of equity investors, I see that some of them were introductions from other contacts of mine, whom I met from someone else. Getting leads for private money gets easier, as long as you keep producing good deals with solid returns for your Cash Providers.

Tier 2 is about leveraging and cultivating relationships in your Core Group to take you to the next level and expand your Cash Provider list. One way you can do this is to go to your savvy investors and speak with them about helping you grow your business. They probably know others like them who are already involved in passive investments. As they say, birds of a feather flock together. As you build the relationship with your Cash Providers, you can ask them whether they know anyone in their circles who also might be interested in being a passive investor. See whether they can make some introductions for you. You could even talk to them about serving as a more permanent adviser to your company and give them a small slice of equity in your deals in exchange for sponsoring your loans with banks, introducing you to investors, or some other role. Remember, their role should not extend beyond helping you raise money because giving away ownership in exchange for fund-raising is a no-no with the SEC.

A few good lead sources for potential Cash Providers are attorneys, CPAs, and financial planners. You don't want to approach them on your first deals, but once you have a track record in place, they can put you in front of their high-net-worth clients. Some financial planners get it, and others don't. The shortsighted ones will see you as a competitor, thinking you will enroll their clients to give most of their funds to you for deals and take it out of their accounts with the financial planner. The ones who get it will see that there is a need for diversification in their clients' investments and that there are products out there that they can't offer. Passive real estate investments offer a real alternative that is not tied to what happens on Wall Street. Financial planners who are really looking out for their clients' best interests may see the benefit of an introduction. Additionally, there are some advisers who are compensated based on their clients' net worth, regardless of where it's held. They don't get fees on which mutual fund or annuity that the client invests in. If the client makes more money, so does the planner. If you find one who's compensated that way, they won't care what investment the money goes into, as long as it's the right move given their client's goals.

Another strategy I would highly recommend is conducting educational presentations for your Core Group and existing Cash Provider circles. Let me explain and provide some examples.

EXAMPLE NO. 1 | Cash Provider Circle

Say you just returned one of your private lender's money back (along with interest) after a fix-and-flip project sold. Your Cash Provider (let's call her Amy) is happy, and so are you. You have developed a good relationship with Amy, and during one of your discussions, you learn that she is active in a local country club. You share with Amy that you are looking for more private lenders, so you ask whether she would help put an event together with you at her country club. Of course, you would pay for any costs associated with this. But the basic premise would be to invite other country club members to an educational presentation about real estate investing and the dos and don'ts about investing passively in real estate. Let me be clear here: This is not an opportunity to "pitch" these members on *anything*; this is merely an opportunity to provide education and knowledge when it comes to the topic of investing passively in real estate. The most effective Deal Providers are always looking for ways to add value by educating and helping others.

EXAMPLE NO. 2 | Core Group Circle

Say you have a business owner (let's call him Bob) whom you have worked with and know very well in your networking circle. This person is part of your Core Group. Now, this Core Group has not invested with you themselves, but they would refer you to people who trust and respect them. Above all, they trust and respect you. During a discussion with Bob, you learn that he runs a local Rotary club. (For those who have never heard of Rotary, it is a philanthropic organization that has 1.2 million members and 35,000 clubs around the world.) During your discussion, you share with Bob that you have a great presentation that you conduct on how to invest in real estate state passively. Bob is intrigued and asks you to come be a speaker for his Rotary club next month.

I recently had the opportunity to present in front of one of my Core Group's Rotary clubs, and this is the exact topic that I presented on: "how to invest passively" in real estate. Again, this was educational, and I discussed the differences between passive and active investors, types of passive investments, and how to choose the right investor. The presentation went great, and there were a few folks who came up to me afterward wanting to connect further. Remember, Tier 2 is all about expanding your current circles and network by tapping into your Core Group's (and existing Cash Providers') networks.

Moving from Tier 1 to Tier 2

Once you begin expanding your circle and receiving referrals, you will need to put tools and systems into place so you can handle more investors, contacts, and deals. Here are a few steps I suggest you take.

Upgrade Your Database

Remember that master list you created to find your Core Group? Most likely you put it together as a simple spreadsheet or even a handwritten list. This is fine to get started, but as you grow, you need to use a professional database/ software to keep track of your current and potential Cash Providers and your Core Group. I find that a good customer relationship management (CRM) software, used by sales reps to keep track of their customers, is the most helpful. The better ones will connect to other apps, like your calendar and your email, for seamless integration. We use Podio because it has a fairly robust free version, but you have to set it up, which requires a bit of up-front time. I've also heard that Pipedrive is good, and if you want to pay for a top-of-the-line product, you can take a look at software like Salesforce, which is used by large companies. The main thing you want is ease of use and the ability to keep track of your progress with each of your current and potential Cash Providers. Regardless of the type of system you use, the key is to organize your contacts and create a process for staying in consistent touch with these individuals.

Crank Up Your Social Media Machine

It may be hard to put out regular social media posts when you are just getting started and haven't done a deal yet. Once you get a few projects under your belt, you need to use social media to your benefit. There are so many creative things you can do. You can post pictures of your properties under renovation and put out some "celebration" posts when you close on a purchase or a sale. You also want to share learned lessons and challenges. This business of investing is not always sunshine and happiness. You want to be as real, authentic, and transparent as possible. You should also create a Facebook, Instagram, or even YouTube page for your business. That way, you are creating something larger than yourself, not centered on you personally but on the real estate empire you are building. People who are willing to subscribe, like, or otherwise follow your social media feed for your business are showing interest in what you do. They could be prospective Cash Providers in the near future, and since they have subscribed to your page, channel, etc., you can put out well-crafted opportunities to work with you.

Consistency Is Key

We have a newsletter we send about once a month with a brief update on all our funds, highlights on a few wins, new opportunities we have in the pipeline, and, most important, real estate investing tips and learned lessons. You want to continually (and consistently) put content out that shows that you know what you are talking about. Above all else, you want to be someone who adds tons of value and is a resource. The CRM we use (Podio) connects to MailChimp (which we use for our newsletter), and when we add a new contact in Podio, it automatically adds him or her to our MailChimp newsletter. We also have a way for individuals to sign up for our newsletter through our website and our YouTube channel. It doesn't matter how many people are in your database to begin with. If you make it easy for people to jump on board and follow what you are up to, they will. We have found many investors who simply discovered us through social media, started following us, and reached out to us to learn more about our company. After building a relationship with them and talking about their goals, they became interested in investment opportunities we had to offer.

A monthly newsletter model serves another purpose as well—it keeps your Core Group and current investors in the loop on what you are up to. Investors don't want to be in the dark on how their money is doing, and they don't want to have to chase you down for updates. In a later chapter, I will discuss investor relations in greater depth. For now, the key for you to consider is what consistent communication you can create to stay in front of your Core Group and potential and current Cash Providers.

Create a Track Record Document

Most new investors are going to want to see what you've done in the past to get comfortable with you. Once you've done a few deals, create a brief summary showing the details of your projects. Make sure you have lots of before-and-after pictures and a summary of the financials for each project. The financial summary should include acquisition and construction costs, value when complete, and, most important, the return on investment that your Cash Provider received from working with you on the project. This establishes your credentials easily with prospects and gives you something to put in front of people right away when you meet with them for the first time. I will discuss this more and even give you a sample in a later chapter. However, I want to get your wheels turning now on this topic.

TIER 3 | Taking It Public

Tier 3   Taking it Public

We have discussed Tier 1, which is your Core Group. Ideally, you have made a list of *everyone* in your Core Group as a result of participating in the "making your master list" task in the above section. Please, please, please stop reading here if you have *not* completed this list. I promise you, if you take this exercise seriously, people you weren't previously thinking of as Cash Providers will come to mind. We have also discussed Tier 2, which are referrals of Tier 1—either referrals of your Core Group of people who like and respect you or referrals of your Cash Providers. Tier 2 was all about expanding your circles, which you can do by getting one-on-one referrals or trying the educational presentation strategy that I shared. Now we are on Tier 3, which is all about taking it public. When I state "taking it public," I am referring to broadcasting your real estate investing business to people who do *not* know you. There are various paths to do this. I am going to review seven of them here.

PATH NO. 1 | Finding Lenders via Public Records

A very common strategy that has been discussed in real estate investing circles (especially in the BiggerPockets forums) is finding private lenders through your county public records. In some counties, you can do this research online. In other counties, you need to go physically to the appropriate county office, such as a clerk's office. The next step is to determine how loans are secured. In our trading area, the loan is secured using a mortgage. In other areas, the loan is secured using a deed in trust. Once you figure out what it is called in your area (deed in trust, mortgage, or something else), you want to look for these documents in public records. You want to find out as much as you possibly can, such as the price the property closed for, the interest rate, and, most important, the lender's name and address.

Once you get this information, there are a lot of strategies you can follow. You can be bold and cold-call them if you do further research to get their phone number. I used to do a lot of cold calling in my early days of sales. It is not the easiest. However, it can yield results if you're determined and consistent. Besides cold calling, you can send these private lenders direct mail. There are tons of best practices when it comes to direct mail, which is not my expertise. Your best bet is to get educated on the most effective strategies on direct mail from various experts out there. If you know any top-notch wholesalers, they will have great suggestions on the latest and greatest techniques when it comes to direct mail.

PATH NO. 2 ▌ Finding Lenders Online

With a Plus or Pro membership, you can post your deals on the BiggerPockets marketplace. When presenting the deal, you always want to provide background information about the deal and the numbers, and if you have a track record, definitely include your experience and a brief overview of the deals you have done. This shows your street cred (i.e., that you have been a good steward of other people's money and can close deals).

Additionally, there are specific websites that focus on connecting lenders with lending opportunities. Just remember to do your due diligence before using any of these websites. I find it helpful to do a quick search in the BiggerPockets search bar before I use a new service or company. If you don't find any feedback there, you can ask about the website you are considering on a forum post. Bottom line: Make sure you know what you are getting into.

PATH NO. 3 ▌ Expanding Your Network

Do you know that adage "You become whom you surround yourself with"? I've found this to be true. As you grow, consider getting into some higher-net-worth circles. If you are the most successful person you know, it's time to meet some new people. Spending time with successful people will cause you to expand your possibilities, inspire you with new ideas, and give you a network that has been through what you are experiencing and can give you some guidance. There are networking groups dedicated to business owners and others who are geared toward those who have achieved a certain level of success in life. If you can find a group that has a barrier to entry based on income, business size, or experience, check it out.

PATH NO. 4 ❙ Becoming a Thought Leader

Once you have been doing this for a while, people will start to come to you as a source of ideas, inspiration, advice, or even help with getting out of a jam. You will be viewed as someone who knows what he or she is doing based on what you've completed already. When that starts to happen, you are moving to another path of Tier 3, which is becoming a Thought Leader. I first heard this term through a mentor of mine, Joe Fairless. He coached my wife and me when we decided to expand our portfolio a few years ago. During one of our coaching calls, he recommended that we step it up and commit to educating others on a larger scale in a very consistent way. He explained that Thought Leaders are people who have earned a little larger megaphone to broadcast their thoughts on the business, success stories, and cautions from their mistakes. There are plenty of people out there broadcasting, but the true Thought Leaders in this business don't just talk about it—they are walking the walk and active in the business also.

Consistency Wins the Race

You will find that your social media efforts will start to pay off as well. You are not going to get 1,000 followers your first week in business, but if you are consistent with it and put out quality content, you will be building a following that will eventually turn into investors. When we started our Landlord's Chronicles YouTube channel a few years ago, we committed to posting two videos a week. We lived by that commitment even through busy times, the holidays, and while on vacation. I don't think we've missed a day since we made the commitment. We also put out quality videos and rarely promoted anything. Ninety-nine percent of the videos are just real-life education, tips, and learned lessons from our projects. Eventually we started a series called "Mentorship Monday," in which subscribers could email us a question to **HelpMe@DeRosaGroup.com**. I would answer the question on the YouTube channel in a five-minute video, shot from the camera on my computer at my office. At the beginning, our subscribership started low, less than a few hundred for six months or so. However, as soon as we committed to producing consistent, valuable content on a biweekly basis, our subscribership began to increase. As a result, our YouTube page continues to grow with new subscribers each day. Some of our investors in a recent project we just funded started off as subscribers to our YouTube channel. To use a race analogy, social media is not a sprint; it's a marathon. If you commit to it, you won't see the payoffs at first, so you have to keep going. Eventually it will snowball and grow exponentially.

Other Outlets to Broadcast Yourself

Creating a YouTube channel is not the only megaphone you can get your hands on. Here are a few others you can tap into:

- **Podcasts** – According to Entrepreneur.com,[2] 68 million Americans listen to podcasts, which is about one in four people across the country. So it's safe to say that podcast listenership is rising and will continue to rise. While I have never started a podcast myself, I have seen firsthand the amount of work and energy that goes into one. My wife recently launched a podcast for women real estate investors called *The Real Estate InvestHER Show* and I saw how hard she worked to launch. She even took a digital course to get it right. Just as with a YouTube channel, you will need to be committed to putting out consistent and quality content, regardless of how many downloads you are getting. Besides starting your own podcast, you can also approach the many podcast hosts out there to try to get on their show as a guest. They are always looking for interesting stories from active investors who are willing to share them. It's a good way to get your name out there, plug your own channel/blog/podcast, and also build a relationship with the host.

- **Blogs** – What better way to be a Thought Leader than to start a blog or even become a regular contributor on someone else's blog? Just like every other venue I have been discussing here, if you start a blog, same thing goes—be consistent and share quality information. Since there are probably millions of blogs on the Internet, you have to be a bit creative and figure out how your blog will stand out from all the others. You can create your own blog on its own platform and hosting site. Or you can take advantage of starting a blog

---

2 Rose Leadem, "The Growth of Podcasts and Why It Matters," *Entrepreneur*, 2017, https://www.entrepreneur.com/article/306174.

on an existing platform. I know people who have had a lot of success with starting a member blog on BiggerPockets. In addition to starting a member blog, you can also offer your opinion and support for the questions posted on the forums. If you offer up your opinion on questions on the forums regularly, people will start to come to you for advice, ideas, and opportunities. Remember, one thing turns into another. If you commit to two blog posts a week and four forum comments a week, you will be on your way to building your thought leadership reputation.

You Never Know Who Is Reading

A number of years ago, I got a call from a fellow investor in Trenton. He said that a reporter for a national magazine was looking to do an article on the Trenton real estate market and wanted to interview three active investors. I agreed and talked to the reporter that week. I didn't think much of it afterward, until I got a call a month later. It was from a doctor in New Jersey. During our discussion, he shared that he was part of a group of thirty doctors who owned practices all over the state. Some of them were looking to get into real estate investing, and as you can guess, they didn't have the time to do it themselves. They asked me to come down to meet with them and soon after committed to investing in our first small apartment building project. I still work with these doctors today. All it took was a thirty-minute phone interview to get connected to them. You never know who's reading.

PATH NO. 5 | Speaking Opportunities

In an earlier chapter, I talked about getting involved with local real estate groups (and business organizations). As you grow into Tier 3, it becomes even more important to get opportunities to give educational presentations for these groups, as well as groups you are not a member of. To figure out which groups would be best for you to speak in front of, you first need to brainstorm where your ideal Cash Providers hang out. For example, maybe you want to begin working with engineers (since you are an engineer yourself). You want to look for any and all membership organizations that cater to engineers in a one-hundred-mile radius of your home. What meetings are held? When are they held? Are there any conferences coming up that you can speak at?

Another side benefit of giving presentations is that your public speaking and presentation skills will improve. If you grow your investor database large enough, you will need to become proficient (even exceptional) at presenting opportunities. Additionally, telling prospective investors that you regularly speak on the topic of investing further establishes you as an industry expert and a Thought Leader.

PATH NO. 6 | Crowdfunding

For those of you who aren't familiar with it, crowdfunding is a way to raise money for your deals through online portals. Investors go online and surf these portals until they find a deal that meets their investment criteria. Until recently, these sights were limited to accredited investors, but there are now options for accredited and nonaccredited investors. The deals on these sites are typically large in size and price and are "interesting" high-profile deals. Just for some inspiration, go out and surf these sites to see what's being offered. Once you have a track record in midsize deals, you can take a shot at putting together a larger deal on one of these sites. Most require a substantial fee to list with them, and they do vet your deal to make sure it's profitable enough for their investor base.

Crowdfunding is new to the scene of real estate investing, but it's here to stay. They are still working out the kinks on who can invest in these deals and how they are regulated, but because there is quite a bit of money to be made in fees for assembling these kinds of deals, I predict that we will see more and more real estate being offered and invested in on these sites in the future. Even if you aren't ready to put anything out there yet, keep an eye on the regulations around this space because when it becomes more mainstream, it will be a game changer when it comes to raising money.

PATH NO. 7 | Private Equity Funds and Equity Brokers

Once you've got a long track record and have taken down a few larger deals, you may find that you want to expand to the next level, beyond investing with your standard Cash Provider and into the space of working with companies, family offices, and brokers whose job it is to go out and find you money for a fee. These cash sources are going to want to see a very long track record and will have specific terms that they will invest into. It becomes less of a give-and-take arrangement, as these are professional investors who know what deal terms work for them. They may want more equity than your individual Cash Providers and may want you to work very hard and get paid very little in the beginning, with a big pay day once the deal is profitable and they have all their money back. In exchange for that, they can cut very big checks and get you into a new arena of deal size.

Final Thoughts on Where to Find Cash Providers

If I have to sum up this chapter in one sentence, I would say: Put one foot in front of the other. I can't stress that enough. Tier 1 is all about those who like, respect, and trust you. Start there. Then progress to Tier 2 and Tier 3. I talk to a lot of new investors, and they want to run before they walk. Not only is this not possible, but it is not smart. When you are investing other people's money, being smart with your decisions is absolutely a must. Let me remind you: You are in a marathon, not a sprint.

As you can tell, I am a big fan of using digital marketing and social media. As a result of this chapter, I invite you to commit to one way you can get your name out there. One thing. Whether you choose to begin blogging or start a YouTube channel or even a podcast, just get started with something, and commit to producing consistent and quality content. I would encourage you to give yourself one year. After a year, you can determine whether the effort is yielding you the results you want. Remember, any of these digital marketing strategies takes time. You will develop a nice database for people to see when they start researching you. And they will.

CHAPTER 6
HOW TO TURN POTENTIAL INTO REALITY

Most of this book has been preparing you for this moment—going out and meeting with potential Cash Providers to present the opportunity to work with you. There is a bit of prep work you need to do before you take the actions laid out here. This chapter will be the most effective for you if you've already created your list of potential money partners as instructed in the previous chapter. If you have not done this, please stop here and do the following activity: Take out a piece of paper and brainstorm your Tier 1 list. I promise that having this list handy will enable you to envision having the conversations described in this chapter with the people on your list. Seeing yourself speaking with these people using the tools I give you here will help you be effective when you move into turning your potential Cash Provider list into reality (the actual Cash Providers lined up for your next project).

Before we begin with the actual process of presenting to potential investors, let's discuss two critical areas.

Fear of Asking for Money

I am sure you would agree that fear is one powerful emotion for us humans. Although fear actually lives in our mind, the experience of fear can feel extremely real in our day-to-day lives. When I began presenting to potential Cash Providers, I certainly experienced fear of asking for money. But here is the thing—you are *not* asking for money. You are providing an investment opportunity. *Let me say this again so you really hear it. You are not asking for money. You are providing an investment opportunity.* Never feel as though you are imposing on people. *You* are providing opportunities for Cash Providers to make a return on their money. And remind yourself as you move through this raising-private-money process: You are helping them just as much as they are helping you. You are *not* a beggar with your hand out, and they are not doing you a favor. You are a real estate investor who is helping Cash Providers achieve their financial goals. You are helping people build their wealth while you build your business. Don't ever forget this.

In my experiences (both personally and professionally), I have learned that the only way to deal with fear is to move through fear, not around it. As a human being, you will always have fear in your life. The key is to not allow it to take over your life and stop you from going out there and raising money for your real estate deals. Dale Carnegie said it best: "Inaction breeds doubt and fear. Action breeds confidence and courage. If you want to conquer fear, do not sit home and think about it. Go out and get busy." By taking action toward your goals of raising private money, you will gain confidence every step of the way. As you gain confidence, you will begin to reduce fear's power over you.

Your Personality ▌ The Good, the Bad, and the Ugly

I started dating my wife many years ago. Ironically, during the same month I started dating her, she began working for a consulting business that was the licensee of a personality assessment tool that analyzed people's behaviors, motivators, strengths, communication style, etc. Needless to say, during the first month of dating Liz, she had me take this personality assessment she was working with. When she first asked me to take the assessment, I thought, Seriously, my new girlfriend wants to analyze me?! After some initial reluctance, I did end up taking the assessment, and I was even interested in seeing the results.

In hindsight, I am so glad that she had me take this assessment. The results told me so much about my own style. It confirmed my personality strengths, and it certainly pointed out my blind spots. If you are going to embark on raising private money and presenting to potential Cash Providers, you must know yourself inside and out. You need to know your strengths and weaknesses. You need to know this information about yourself so you can *adapt* your style to potential Cash Providers. There are some potential Cash Providers whom you are going to hit it off with and others who will be a challenge to connect with. Either way, you need to have a lot of self-awareness. These personality type assessments can answer questions such as:

Are you more of a detail person?

Are you a risk taker?

Are you more of a big-picture person?

Are you more analytical and task oriented?

Are you more relationship driven and people focused?

Do you under-communicate?

Do you over-communicate?

Are you too direct with people? Or not direct enough?

Do you move too quickly with decisions? Or not quick enough?

Do you jump into new situations quickly? Or do you take your sweet time?

You might "know" these things about yourself already, but what I love about taking these assessments is that they offer an *objective* perspective of you. For example, it is not a surprise to anyone I work with that I am more of a people person. I am also more of a big-picture person. Like you, I have strengths and I have areas of my personality that have gotten me into sticky situations. You need to be crystal clear on your weaknesses and then manage these weaknesses. Most important, you need to adapt to the potential Cash Providers you are talking to and meeting with. Remember, they are not just investing in a deal; they are first and foremost investing in you. To invest in you, they need to trust you.

Here are some general ways you can adapt to various potential Cash Providers:

Extrovert/Introvert

- If you are more of an extroverted person and you are meeting with a more introverted person, you need to tone your style down. You can overtalk, and this introverted Cash Provider will not trust you. Get to the point, and don't chitchat too much with this type of person.
- If you are more of an introverted person and you are meeting with a more extroverted person, you need to engage in more chitchat with him or her. You will want to get right to the point, but if the provider is more extroverted, he or she will want to get to know you first.

Quick/Methodical

- If you are more of a fast-paced type of person and you are meeting with a more methodical person, then you might move through the deal and presentation too quickly. Slow down and remember not to rush.
- If you are more of a methodical person, you might move too slowly for very fast-paced people. The greatest thing you can do with any potential Cash Provider is to be very clear and up front with how much time each other has before you begin your meeting.

Detail/Big Picture Oriented

- If you are a detail-oriented person and you are meeting with a big-picture type of person, then you need to tone down the amount of detail you give this potential Cash Provider. The best way to approach this is to give a high-level overview of the deal and then back it up with more detail if the provider seems interested and/or wants more information.
- On the other hand, if you are more of a big-picture person and you are meeting with a more detail-oriented person, you need to be aware that you will not provide this person with nearly enough detail. If you go too general with detail-oriented people, you can appear unprepared and disorganized. Again, having both a high-level overview of the deal and a more detailed overview will be your best bet to serve both types of people.

In summary, there are so many of these personality assessments out in the market. I have taken many of them, and each one has provided me with a different point of view and insight. Take a few different assessments. Learn from them, and use these tools to sharpen up your influencing style. Some that I recommend include the Predictive Index Behavioral Assessment, Kolbe A Index, and CliftonStrengths Assessment.

The Cash Provider Enrollment Process

As you begin to schedule face-to-face meetings with some of these potential Cash Providers, your nervousness will most likely increase. And that makes sense. Nervousness is just a light version of fear, and getting nervous before these meetings is actually a great thing. It's an indicator that whatever you are about to do is important to you. Use it to prepare yourself for this meeting. Let it fuel you to take that meeting seriously.

Preparation

After creating your list of potential Cash Providers, the next step is to begin scheduling meetings with these individuals. Yes, you can schedule phone appointments with them, but I have found when it comes to subjects like raising money, it is best that these discussions are done face-to-face. If the potential Cash Provider is not close to where you are located, then at least use video conferencing.

Regardless, you want to be as prepared as possible before meeting with this potential investor. There are five critical areas you want to be prepared with before you step into the meeting.

- Your Goals
- Your Marketing Brochure
- Your Track Record
- Deals Analysis
- WIIFM

Your Goals – Where do you see yourself going?

By no means do you want to launch into your goals as the *first* discussion item with potential Cash Providers. But at some point in the conversation, you want to weave in your goals and where you are headed in your business. Some of the questions you can prepare for:

- What goals do you have for your real estate business in the next one to three years?
- What kinds of deals are you going to focus on/do you focus on?
- What types of infrastructure will you be implementing over the years to achieve your goals?

Marketing Brochure – Why should they invest with you?

The biggest question that these potential Cash Providers are going to ask themselves and you need to answer for them is "Why should they invest with *you?*" Something I created that has been very valuable over the years is what I call the marketing brochure. This is a one-page summary that explains:

- Who you are and your experience (types of deals you have done and the successes you have had)
- How Cash Providers have worked with you in the past and the returns they got
- Benefits of working with you

- Testimonials (from other investors and/or colleagues who have worked with you)

Your Track Record

One of the most important ways to prove yourself to potential Cash Providers is to share with them your track record. Ultimately these potential investors care about *one thing*. They care about the protection of their money. Yes, they care about making a return on their money, but they care most about getting their money back from you. The greatest way you can prove to them that you will take good care of their investment is to show them your track record. You need to show them the types of deals you have done, the timeline, the costs, and, most important, the profit. They want to see what type of projects you have done so that they feel more comfortable investing with you.

I would suggest creating a handout (or a few, ideally) that includes before-and-after pictures of each project, along with as many details as possible. Here are some suggestions on what to include in the track record handout:

- Project type (fix-and-flip, small rental, apartment, etc.)
- Property information (i.e., location, bedrooms, bath, square feet, units)
- Purchase price
- Rehab cost
- After-repair value or sale price
- Profit on sale (flip) or monthly cash flow (rental)
- Project timeline (from purchase to sale or refinance, including milestones like the time it took to renovate, days on market for a flip, and time to lease out for a rental)
- Cash provider investment
- Cash provider profit/return (this translates to the annual ROI)

Here is an example of the information I included in one of our track record documents from a fix-and-flip project in Philadelphia. Since we do not live super close to the project, we decided to set up a joint venture agreement with local partners on this project.

PROPERTY INFO 2 BEDS, 2.5 BATHS 1,600 SQ FT FINISHED BASEMENT	
Purchase Price	$114,000
Rehab + Carrying Costs	$119,000
Project Timeline	Six months
Under Contract	One day
Sold Price	$339,900
Commission + Closing Costs	$25,000
Profit	$81,900

Deal Analysis – Do you know your deal inside and out?

During your meeting with a potential Cash Provider, you want to review and have prepared a couple of examples of the types of deals you would like to raise money for. These can be fix-and-flip and/or buy-and-hold opportunities. These can be real deals that are active on the market (or not active), as long as they are good examples of the types of projects that you will be raising private money for. These examples should provide as closely estimated numbers as possible, including all the financials such as income and expenses, a brief story on the deal itself, and the potential return that the Cash Provider can make if he or she works with you. We use the calculators on the BiggerPockets website. These tools allow us to break down our numbers in a simple and understandable way for our potential money partners, and they also allow us to insert before-and-after pictures. If you haven't tried them already, check them out.

WIIFM

Do you know what everyone's favorite radio station is? No, it is not a jazz station, rap station, classical station, or even talk-radio station. It is WIIFM, which stands for "What's in it for me?" Although I tend to believe people are good by nature and really do care about one another, I also believe that when you present something to anyone about *anything*, the first thought that pops into the person's head is "What's in it for me?"

Potential Cash Providers want to know how the information you are presenting to them is going to affect them. Potential Cash Providers want to know how to protect their money and how they are going to get out of the deal. Now, in most situations, potential Cash Providers are not going to actually ask you what's in it for them. Some very direct and bottom-line-oriented people might ask this question. But in most situations, people are not going to be that bold. However, every single potential Cash Provider will at least be thinking about this. So as the Deal Provider, you need to be ahead of the Cash Provider. Before you step foot into the meeting with potential Cash Providers, you need to be 100 percent prepared. You need to be ready to answer these questions for each potential Cash Provider:

1. What would be the greatest benefit to working with you?
2. What do you think the greatest objection will be?
3. Based on your current knowledge of this person, which investment vehicle would suit him or her best?

The more prepared you are *before* meeting with a potential Cash Provider, the better the meeting will go. Additionally, you will find yourself feeling more comfortable, less nervous, and more confident as you walk into this meeting.

As we come to a close with this section, you might be feeling a bit over-whelmed and saying to yourself, "Wow, that is *a lot* to prepare." I promise you that the more you are prepared, *really* prepared, as you meet with potential Cash Providers, the better these meetings will go for you. Remember, you are asking people to invest with you. It is your responsibility to be as prepared as possible so you don't waste their time and your time. The good news is that once you create these handouts, like your marketing brochure and track record samples, you can use these over and over again.

Scheduling the Meeting

I am sure I don't need to tell you that people are busy. Now more than ever. There is so much competing for our attention on a daily and moment-to-moment basis. We are getting pulled in a million directions on a daily basis—from professional responsibilities to personal responsibilities. The point is that your potential Cash Providers are also getting pulled in a million directions. They will have to believe there is something in it for them to meet with you and give you their undivided attention.

Over the years, I've found a few strategies that have helped me meet with potential Cash Providers:

1. Be persistent and tenacious but not pushy. Everyone appreciates a tenacious person. However, no one appreciates when that tenacity turns into pushiness. It is a fine line, and you have to master this to be an effective influencer.
2. Face-to-face is always the preferred method of influencing people. In this digital world, we forget how important these interactions really are. Second to face-to-face meetings is using some type of video conferencing technology.
3. Don't give up. If these potential Cash Providers are interested in meeting with you but don't immediately get back to you, you need to set up a follow-up system to stay in front of them. I am not recommending you call them every day—that would be harassment. I am suggesting you stay in front of them and follow up in a timeframe that is appropriate.
4. Add these potential Cash Providers (once you have reached out to them and made a connection) to your digital/social media marketing strategies. Remember, with everything competing for their attention, you need to set up consistent ways to stay in touch with them and stay in front of them. Below is an example of how staying in touch with a potential Cash Provider benefited our business in the long run.

Always Stay in Touch

One of my very first Cash Providers lived in New York City, which is often called the center of the financial universe. Many of the people associated with the center of the financial universe are either high-paid professionals or savvy investors, so I approached him to help me find additional Cash Providers. One of the first introductions he made was to a woman who lived in the same building as he did. She already had some investments of her own and even owned and managed a few rentals in the city. We sat down for coffee for the first meeting, and I was prepared with my track record document, marketing material, and even a few deals ready for funding. We never got to any of that. Within the first five minutes of the meeting, it came up that Liz and I were expecting our first baby, and we talked about the pregnancy, parenting, and raising children for an hour. I let her drive the conversation. I could tell it would take some time to build a relationship to establish trust, and I was fine with that. The next visit, we sat and talked about her past, how she got to New York City, and more about parenting. I called her a few times to check in, and we chatted, but she kept deferring the conversation away from investments and wanted to talk about how my wife was doing (at this point, we had already had the baby!). I was patient and let it go for a while, calling or e-mailing every few weeks. For our third face-to-face meeting, she came to visit me at my office in Trenton and wanted to look at some projects we had in development. We were getting warmer. I told her about returns our past investors had made, and at the end of that meeting, she committed $100,000 to our next project.

The Meeting – Avoid Throwing Up

Earlier in the chapter, I encouraged you to increase your understanding of your strengths and weaknesses (or, as I like to call them, areas to watch out for). With this additional insight into yourself, I am sure these meetings will go even more effectively for you. I want to encourage you to become more aware of Cash Providers' behavior within the first few minutes of the meeting. In other words, you can tell a lot about people's personality by their body language, their tonality, and the words they use. For example, if the potential Cash Provider looks impatient and is using very few words with you, then he or she is probably more of a bottom-line person. You want to adapt your style to the provider's and get to the point as quickly as possible. If the potential Cash Provider seems more relaxed and chatty, then adapt your style accordingly. Bottom line: You want to become a master of people, a master of adapting your style to meet the needs of the person you are meeting in some way.

Here are few recommendations for an effective meeting:

1. Thank Cash Providers for meeting with you. Don't ever take for granted people's time. Be appreciative of it.
2. Listen. Really listen to potential Cash Providers. Don't just wait for your turn to talk, but truly listen to what they are saying. As they say, we were given two ears and one mouth for a reason. We should be listening more than talking.
3. Ask questions about them. You need to learn what their interest in real estate investing is. You need to learn what their investing goals are. You need to learn about their financial goals. You need to understand the "why" behind their financial and investing goals.
4. Once you understand their goals and interest, you can *weave in* your recent real estate investing activity. You want to share the types of projects you have done. You want to share your recent successes. And you want to share that you are looking for someone to help you grow your business as you help them grow their wealth.

5. Avoid throwing up on them. Not literally, of course—that would be awful! I mean figuratively. So many people in these types of situations walk into the meeting and then just start talking about themselves and the deals they have done, and go *on and on* about themselves and how great they are. Please, do not do this. Yes, you will need to share your successes with them, but you need to ask some questions and seek to understand them first before you can begin talking about investing with you.

SUCCESS·TIP   *In Stephen Covey's 7 Habits of Highly Effective People, habit number five is "seek to first understand and then to be understood." Let's be honest. Most people in conversations and meetings are waiting for their turn to talk. They are not listening with the intention to really listen. So many of us want to make sure our point comes across, and as a result, we miss what people say. Most of us took classes in school for reading, writing, and public speaking. However, most of us did not take any classes on listening. The conversations in which I actually practice this—seek to first understand, then to be understood—go so much more smoothly. Most important, the person you are communicating with really feels understood and appreciated, which is an incredibly important human need.*

I can't stress listening to your potential money partners enough. If you ask the right questions and listen to the answers, they will tell you exactly where they will fit into your business if they are interested. They may not come out and say, "I'd love to lend you money on your next fix-and-flip project with my self-directed IRA!" They probably won't come out and tell you, but if you listen, they will leave some clues about how their goals align with your investing goals. Here are some signals to look for:

Private Lender Signals
As I highlighted in an earlier chapter, self-directed IRAs are an incredible investment vehicle for both the Deal and Cash Providers. Anytime you encounter people who have more than $50,000 in their IRA, they are a potential

Cash Provider for you. All you need to do is show them the benefits.

Aside from SDIRA holders, you may encounter a prospect who simply wants fixed income and security. Remember, a private loan has a fixed return with collateral to protect the investment. Some potential private lenders will want security and predictability above all else. They will want to preserve their wealth and may be willing to take a lower return in exchange for security. A private loan with a monthly payment can be a means of providing fixed income for those who are retired and live on other sources of fixed income, such as a pension or Social Security.

Others may want to test you out first. A savvy investor may want to "date until you get married" on a small, short-term project before committing to something larger with a long timeline. A private loan can be a good way to establish yourself with this investor to show you have integrity and can be trusted with his or her capital long term. Some of my largest Cash Providers started out with a small investment in the form of a private loan for $50,000. Soon after, they were putting hundreds of thousands into apartment building deals with me.

Private Equity Signals

If *income* and *security* are the buzzwords for private lenders, then the words for equity investors are things like *tax benefits, wealth building,* and *alternative investments.* These are the people who will say, "I wish I could invest in real estate, but I just don't have the time." Equity investors most likely already see the benefits of investing in real estate; they just need to get educated on how the deals with you get structured.

Most of my equity investors in rental deals are high-paid professionals or savvy investors, as the benefits of these types of long-term projects are slanted in their favor. The tax benefits specifically greatly benefit high-paid professionals, who are very sensitive to income tax. You should lead with tax benefits in conversations with these types of investors. If you plan on offering ownership equity in your fix-and-flips through joint venture structures, you may do well offering that to those with SDIRAs. As you may recall, they are not liable to pay capital gains tax on their profits, which greatly increases their returns. This may be very appealing to investors who have these vehicles but are open to taking more risks in exchange for a larger return.

The Most Common Cash Provider Questions

I've been doing this for a while and have found that most potential Cash Providers have the same questions. Although the questions are the same, how you answer them is very important. Your answer can lead to a deal in the pipeline, or it could kill the opportunity. Here are the most common questions I hear from prospects and how I typically answer them.

Q: How and when am I going to get my money back?
A: If you don't answer this one the right way, you are done. You need to have a clear and concise path to the return of their capital for them to feel comfortable working with you. For a flip, you want to clearly outline the sales process and explain that their mortgage on the property gets paid off when the property sells. For a rental deal, have your exit strategy lined up. This will most likely be a sale or refinance of the property, but be prepared to go into that in detail and tell them exactly when you plan to get them out.

Q: What are the risks?
A: Don't pull any punches or soften things up on this one. Tell them that there are risks associated with investing. The rental market could crash, tenants could stop paying their rent (which will lower or eliminate cash flow), the flip may not sell right away, interest rates may go up, and on and on. You want to tell them clearly what the most likely downsides are and how probable they may be. Most important, tell them what you are doing to mitigate and avoid those risks. Show that your fix-and-flip is going to be listed for 5 percent below the current market price. Show them that you have a vacancy rate included in your rental projections. Ideally, you've thought of these risks already and have a plan to work around them. Show them your plan.

Q: How much of your own money are you putting in?
A: This question gets asked quite a bit, so be prepared for it. If you are putting your own cash in, bring this up early, and it will cut through many of their other concerns. Investors love to see that you are willing to put your money where your mouth is and see your coinvestment as a sign of your belief in the deal. If you are not investing alongside them, that's OK too. Please don't respond to it with "Well, I don't have any money, so I'm not putting in anything!" Even if you aren't investing in the deal, you need to frame this properly for your investors to accept that. Show them the amount of work

you are going to do to keep the deal moving. It's called sweat equity, and it's of value. If you are going to borrow money from a bank on the deal, you are most likely going to have to personally guarantee that loan, which is a major contribution. If they see the value of your involvement in the deal, they can look past how much cash you have in it.

Q: What if I need my money back?

A: First, you need to educate your Cash Providers that most real estate investments are not liquid, meaning it's very hard to get the cash back quickly. They should not be putting money into deals with you that they may need for something else anytime soon. Real estate investing takes time, and it rarely goes exactly according to plan. They probably won't be able to get the money back until the project is complete, unless you can find someone to "buy" their position from them and take their place. If you sense that your investors are giving you their last dime of cash and aren't giving themselves any cushion for unexpected things with their personal expenses, it's your duty to say something about it.

Q: How does this affect my income taxes?

A: If they haven't invested before, you will need to explain that the money they make with you is taxable. Tell them that they will be getting a 1099 from you for interest on the loans you have with them and a K-1 for any partnerships they have with you. You need a good CPA on your team before you jump into these deals. A good CPA will make this process easy for your investors and may even be willing to explain the process to them.

Q: What are the logistics?

A: This question is never worded the same, but in general, your Cash Providers will want to know the details on how they get the money to you, how it's protected, and the legal documents that set things up. If they have an IRA, be prepared to hold their hand to get the money over to an IRA custodian. They likely won't know how to do this; you will have to teach them. If they've never lent money before, explain how mortgages work and what a lien is. If it's an equity deal, explain what an operating agreement is and how it protects them. Make sure they understand how all the I's are dotted and T's are crossed so they are clear. If they aren't, this process will seem complicated and could scare them off.

They will surely ask you more questions than these, and all investors and their concerns are different. Be prepared for lots of questions in general. The more they ask, the better. Don't be afraid to tell them that you need to get more information before you give them an answer. The worst thing you can do is shoot from the hip, make something up, or tell them what you think they want to hear.

Follow-up ❙ Where Most Deal Providers Fall Off

First, congrats! You got through the first meeting with your potential Cash Providers. That is a huge win for you. It is a win because you are taking action on your goals and taking action to build your investing business as you build other people's wealth. Let's be honest, many of us are not the best at follow-up. We are great in the moment—during the meeting or during the activity—but most of us fall short with follow-up and follow-through. There are only three ways these meetings can go. Let's talk about each of them and then a strategy:

1. Cash Provider is interested in working with you. Great news—now what?! You need to get a deal that meets his or her goals (and yours) and agree on terms. In the next chapter, I am going to go in depth on negotiating terms and necessary paperwork to actually structure the deal. But keep in mind that you want to find a potential deal sooner than later. If someone expresses interest in January and you don't find a deal to present until August, how is that going to look? Ideally, you should have a few deals that you are considering to immediately present to a Cash Provider.

2. Cash Provider is not interested in working with you. I hate to break the bad news to you, but not everyone you meet with is going to want to give you a million dollars. And that is OK. Becoming one of your Cash Providers is not going to be a good fit for everyone. If you have a good relationship with this person but he or she is not interested in being a Cash Provider for you, then the person can still help you. If the provider trusts and likes you, he or she can probably help you make introductions to other potential Cash Providers. Don't ever miss the chance to ask for help and whether a Cash Provider knows anyone in his or her circle who could potentially be interested in being your private lender or equity partner.

3. Cash Provider is not interested in working with you *now*. In most cases, this will be the answer. Unless your Cash Provider has the capital

sitting in his or her bank account ready for investment, these relationships typically take time to cultivate. Remember, a "not now" is not a "no." You are in this game of real estate investing for the long term. Real estate investing is not a sprint; it is a marathon. It's fine if the timing is not right for a Cash Provider immediately. You want the timing to be good for the two of you, not just yourself. Most important, you need to put a consistent process and system in place to stay in touch with a Cash Provider so you're not out of sight, out of mind.

Final Thoughts on Turning Potential into Reality

Just like any other sales activity, you have to count your no's until you get to a yes. Don't get discouraged. When people tell you they aren't interested, ask for feedback. People who tell you no can actually give you the most help because they can tell you what you need to do to get their interest. You may find that they are a no for now and a yes in the future. Remember that this is long-term relationship building. Some investors will need to know you for years before working with you.

Don't ever forget the level of responsibility you are taking on in working with other people's money. Never take it for granted or treat it without the utmost and highest level of respect. If you do the right thing every time, word will get around that you are someone who can be trusted, and referrals will come regularly. It's very hard to overcome a bad reputation in this business. It's easier to do the right thing every time, without exception. This is how you truly grow your investor relationships.

CHAPTER 7
HOW TO STRUCTURE THE PRIVATE LOAN DEAL

So you've made all the right moves and didn't skip a step. You checked all the boxes for your prerequisites, found a deal, made your list of Cash Providers, and made the presentation, and they said *yes*! So now what? You are at the point where the rubber meets the road, structuring the deal using a private loan. This is the point that can make or break you in working with private money, so don't take it lightly.

It's also the point that many new investors want to fast-forward to when they first get started. I've talked to brand-new investors who want to know how to set up a syndication for an equity deal or want a copy of my loan documents for my private lenders. There is a reason this is not the first chapter of the book, and that's because the structure is not the first conversation you need to have with your prospects. They will want to know about it but not before talking about you, the deal, and their goals.

In this chapter (and the next one, which will focus on structuring private equity·deals), I'm going to give you an overview on how to set your deals up, but I need to remind you here that I am not an attorney, and the guidance I give you here should not take the place of legal advice. Please don't go cheap and get some of the documents we will talk about here—like a mortgage document or an operating agreement—free off the Internet. You can easily find them, but they are worth what you paid for them: nothing.

I highly recommend a short-term private loan as your first vehicle for investment with your Cash Providers. They are easier to comprehend, and they have a predictable beginning, middle, and end. They are also a good way for you and a new investor to learn about each other until you do a longer deal. If you are a newer investor, you may find it more comfortable to do a short-term project with your Cash Providers at first to get used to working with other people's money.

Setting these up is not too complicated, but the documents that go into them will vary from state to state, as will the lender's rights if you default on the loan. This is yet *another* reason you should consult with an attorney when you set up these deals for the first time. You can ask your attorney to get you the loan documents in a reusable format, like Microsoft Word, so that you can use them on the next deal and it's a onetime expense.

Deciding on the Terms of the Loan

Before you set up the loan documents to get things moving, there are a few key questions you need to ask, the answers to which will help you determine the terms of the loan. Let them guide you to a structure that will benefit both parties.

QUESTION NO. 1 | Who is lending you the money, and where is it coming from?

It may sound funny, but just because someone agreed to lend you money for a deal doesn't mean the money will come from him or her. You need to know who the actual lender is to draw up the loan documents. If the person is lending through an SDIRA, the lender will be something like "XYZ Company, Custodian for Jane Smith, IRA number 123456." If you are working with a savvy investor, the person may be operating through an LLC or another entity, not himself or herself personally.

Cash Providers operating through an SDIRA will most likely not be taking monthly payments from you, as they can't touch the money anyway. On the other hand, people lending you money from an equity line on their home or other piece of real estate will have a monthly expense to maintain that mortgage payment, so they will most likely want a monthly payment from you. I always offer a higher rate if we don't have to make monthly payments, as this is of value to us because I don't have to set aside that monthly interest payment out of our business cash flow. I will give an additional 2 percent interest in most cases if I can pay all the interest back when the loan is repaid.

Not every lender is OK with this, but it's worth asking.

QUESTION NO. 2 | What's the deal?

Along with the source of the Cash Provider's capital, the other factor that will most likely govern most of your loan structure will be the type of investment vehicle you are providing. Considering the source of the Cash Provider's money will help you make sure that he or she wins on the transaction. That said, you have to win too. The loan terms have to allow you an easy path to profit if you can stick to your plan for the project.

I most commonly use private loans on fix-and-flips and on the BRRRR method and usually with an SDIRA as the cash source. Outside the previously discussed benefits of the SDIRA for the Cash and Deal Providers, the other reason I try to keep the money short term is simple. The money is expensive. The rates are high, so I treat a short-term loan like a hot potato: I try not to hold it for too long.

That being said, there are times when I've used these loans on a stable rental deal that has some cash flow. My strategy on these deals is to hold the property until I can assemble some others like it and do a blanket mortgage on a handful of deals with a local bank. I've found that local banks don't care too much about a loan for $50,000 on a row home rental in Trenton, New Jersey. Their tone changes when I assemble ten of these houses and come to them wanting to borrow $500,000. In those cases, I will agree to make monthly payments to the Cash Provider and hold the property until I get my portfolio built. I don't want to have all that interest pile up on the loan, so I make the monthly payment, which is not a problem, since the property is rented or can be rented very easily.

QUESTION NO. 3 | How quickly do I need to close?

I find that, at times, what benefits me most is not the cost of the money; it's how quickly I can close. If you've been around for a while, you know that the best fix-and-flips or small rental deals go to the buyers who can close the fastest. I closed on a few purchases in the same week that I put them under contract with a Cash Provider who understood how to close quickly and trusted us. In those circumstances, I am willing to pay a slightly higher interest rate to get the deal closed.

There are other deals in which the money is at work for a short period of time, and it becomes less of a conversation on interest rate and more of a concern of total cost of the money versus profit in the deal. I once agreed to pay 15 percent annual interest plus three origination points on a loan of $100,000 because I needed the money for only four months.

The total cost of the money was:

15 percent divided by twelve
multiplied by four months
plus 3 percent in points
which equals $8,000 for the money.

The deal involved a six-unit building we purchased for $90,000, and it needed $10,000 in renovations and closing costs. I had a buyer lined up for $150,000 once the work was completed and was glad to pay the interest to get the deal done quickly. It was important to make sure my buyer was serious because that loan was costing me $1,250 per month. If the buyer backed out, I could be stuck with that high monthly payment, looking for another buyer.

QUESTION NO. 4 **|** How much construction is involved?

On the other side of the equation are the longer-term heavy construction deals. When I say heavy construction, I mean that the construction costs are typically as much as if not more than what you paid for the property. On those, a higher interest rate can sink your project. It's hard to predict how long a large construction project will take. There are so many variables that can affect your final completion date. Anything from the weather to issues with permits to your contractor falling off schedule can push your deal back months. In circumstances in which the construction costs of a project are more than the purchase price, you want to try to negotiate a construction draw program with your lender to keep interest costs down.

A construction draw program breaks down like this:
- The Cash Provider commits to lend a certain amount toward the purchase and a separate amount toward construction.
- The Deal Provider produces a project timeline showing construction milestones, with how much money the Cash Provider agrees to inject each time a milestone is reached. Milestones can be something like "all demolition and rough wiring complete" or "drywall hung and trim installed."
- The Deal Provider may want to borrow a small amount of money on top of the purchase price to get started on construction.

- The Cash Provider agrees to hold the remaining money readily accessible within short notice; a week is typical.
- When the Deal Provider reaches a defined milestone in the project, the Cash Provider releases the next round of capital, which is called a construction draw.
- To confirm that the Deal Provider hit the milestone, he or she can offer the Cash Provider a walk-through of the property to see the work. I typically do this with a private YouTube video, which I email to my lenders.
- Some Cash Providers will want interest on the money in escrow while it's waiting for deployment into your deal. Hard money lenders always want this. I try to negotiate this point because Cash Providers can reasonably have the money in some other interest-bearing vehicle with enough liquidity that they can get it for you when you need it. If your Cash Provider insists on something on the money, offer the full interest rate on what has been handed to you for the deal and a discounted rate on what's in escrow. In the past, we settled at half the rate for the money in escrow, which was a good compromise.

A construction draw program works well for the Cash Provider because giving you all the money up front is a risk. Let's say that the purchase price is $50,000, but the renovation work costs an additional $75,000. If the Cash Provider were to give you all the money up front, he or she would be giving you $125,000 on an asset that's worth only $50,000. If you go belly-up halfway through the project, the Cash Provider would be left with a property worth nowhere near what he or she has lent on it. If the Cash Provider uses a construction draw program, he or she can give you the money incrementally, as you add value to property through your construction efforts. If you can't finish the deal for whatever reason, the provider could take the project over from you and finish it with what's sitting in the escrow account. It gives the Cash Provider a hedge in case you fail and also some control over the project if he or she doesn't like the way the renovations are going.

I had a friend who lent money into a fix-and-flip deal and used a construction draw to distribute the loan. The Deal Provider was a bit new to the game, but my friend wanted to give him a shot. About halfway through, the lender did a walk-through inspection after the Deal Provider claimed to hit a milestone. It became evident during the walk-through that the Deal Provider was being taken advantage of by his contractor. Work for the current milestone was not 100 percent complete and looked sloppy, but the contractor had been

100 percent paid out. It came up that the contractor didn't pull permits either, which would be a problem when putting the house up for sale. Fortunately, my friend had some experience and had done plenty of flips on his own. He stepped in and helped the Deal Provider turn the project around with a new contractor who was able to correct the sloppy work, pull permits, and finish the house. From what I heard, they made money on the sale and still do deals together today.

Construction draw loans can also benefit the Deal Provider. If you think about it, you don't need all the money up front, so why pay interest on it? You are most likely going to pay your contractor in phases, so why not wait to borrow the money until you need it and reduce interest costs? Additionally, I have found that these types of loans create both discipline and a sense of urgency to get the project done quickly. If you have only so much money to get through a certain phase of the project, it will make you want to push your contractor to get that phase done quickly. These loans have the lowest interest exposure for the Deal Provider, and as long as you have your systems in place, they can be the best way to go for a medium to large construction project.

I find these questions point me in the right direction, and they help me avoid setting up a deal that could create a potential detriment to me or the Cash Provider. Perhaps there are more questions you want to consider, and that's fine. Remember to focus on what is most important as you begin to structure the terms of a private loan: your Cash Provider's money, goals, and benefits, as well as your own.

Private Loan Pitfalls

Just as there are many questions you need to ask to point you in the right direction when structuring the terms of a private loan, there are things that put too much risk on you or the Cash Provider. Let's call these the private loan pitfalls. I've done a few of these in my earlier years and can tell you that you should avoid them if you can.

PITFALL NO. 1 I Loan Origination Points and Fees for Renewal

A point is a fee for originating the loan, typically due to the lender when he or she issues you the loan. One point equals 1 percent of the loan amount, so three points on a $50,000 loan is $1,500. Some lenders will allow you to pay the points at the end, when the loan is repaid, but most like them paid up front.

Points are a backdoor way for a lender to increase the cost of a loan without charging more interest. If you borrow money at 12 percent for six months and pay two points at closing, your cost of the money is 12 percent divided by six months, which equals 6 percent interest *plus* 2 percent, which is 8 percent for six months and translates into 16 percent annually. The shorter the loan, the more these points drive up the total cost of the money. The longer the loan is, the less they have an effect. That's why I'm OK paying them on longer-term deals, like loans from banks on stable rental properties or larger construction projects that will take a year or more.

Another term that lenders may try to include in their loan agreement is maturity date on the loan, with a fee to renew the loan if you go past that date. The fee is normally between 0.5 to 1 percent of the loan amount and will push back the loan maturity date for a set period. I've accepted this on many of my loans, but I make sure that the project is targeted to be complete well before the maturity date. Be cautious of these types of fees, especially if you are a newer investor. Things rarely go as planned on a renovation project—even when you are a seasoned vet—and for newbies, there will be plenty of unexpected surprises that will push back their timeline and cause them to go into default on a loan with a short maturity date.

Make sure to read your loan documents carefully, especially the what-ifs around your loan going over on time. I've seen loan agreements that automatically go into default if you go over time, meaning that the lender can increase the interest rate dramatically and also begin the foreclosure process. I will typically look at my actual timeline for the project and double that time allotment in the loan agreements. If I think I can get the deal done in six months, I will try to get the loan terms locked in for twelve months.

Let's take a minute to make a comparison here. Things like points and fees are more common with hard money lenders, which should not be confused with private money lenders. Hard money lenders *love* to charge points. Some charge between three and five points, plus their interest rate, which is in the mid-teens. They will also limit your loan to six months or less, and if you go over that time limit, they will charge you more fees to renew the loan. Don't get me wrong—hard money has its place and is necessary for new investors who are looking to ramp up. I've used hard money many times, when I'm in a pinch or need to close quickly. That said, dealing with a private money lender whom you are looking to build a long-term relationship with should not be as expensive as hard money. It has to be a win-win, and paying these types of fees and points is not a win for you—at all.

PITFALL NO. 2 | Monthly Payments on Fix-and-Flips

Just as it is in any business, cash flow is king in real estate investing. If you are doing a rental deal, you have a steady stream of revenue coming from the property once it's leased and you can swing a monthly payment to your lender. If you are doing a fix-and-flip, you don't have any monthly revenue coming in. You don't make any profit at all until the property sells, which can be six months to a year from the day you buy it and take on a loan from a Cash Provider.

Although monthly payments can be a risk for Deal Providers, they may be the only way to make things work for your Cash Providers. If their cash source is real estate through a HELOC, they have a monthly payment to maintain. They may also be relying on a monthly payment from their investments to cover their living expenses. Cash Providers may also be developing trust for you and want to get that monthly check as a confirmation of your financial health. For whatever reason, some Cash Providers won't do a deal without it. I've done plenty of deals with monthly payments, and even though it's not something I will offer up front, it can be done under the right structure.

If you agree to making a monthly payment on your fix-and-flip, it has to come from one of three places (which has drawbacks). The first is your own pocket, which may not be a problem if you are running only one deal at a time. But as you scale up, this can start to be a large check each month.

The second place to get that monthly payment is another deal that has cash flow. You can take the revenue off one of your rentals and maintain expenses on a fix-and-flip, for example. I am not a big fan of this idea either, as it's robbing Peter to pay Paul, meaning you are taking one successful project and maintaining another with it. What if you have a vacancy in that rental and don't make any cash flow that month? There are a lot of what-ifs I can throw out there in this scenario.

The third way to fund the money for a monthly payment is to put it in the budget for the deal up front. Say you have a monthly interest payment of $1,000 to make, and you project the deal to take six months from purchase to sale, so you set aside $6,000 in your budget. You take that cash and put it aside in a savings account, taking $1,000 out each month to make the debt payment. This scenario can work OK for you, as long as nothing goes wrong on your flip. If you go over time, you need to find that cash to keep the debt payment current. Let's say you are flipping a house and find out that you need to waterproof the basement. This will cost you $6,000 and add one month to your timeline. You have $3,000 in contingency, so you need to find another

$3,000 to complete the work, but you also need to chip in $1,000 for an additional month's interest. Anytime something comes up on your deal, you need to account for not only the cost of additional construction work but also more interest-carrying costs. If you are going to do monthly payments, this is the only way I suggest you do it, but you need to set aside a larger contingency for construction. I would also create an interest reserve that is double what you project you will need to be safe.

PITFALL NO. 3 I Prepayment Penalties and Guaranteed Minimums

You will see many banks charge a prepayment penalty on a long-term loan, as you would also see on a buy-and-hold rental purchase. A prepayment penalty is a fee that lenders get to charge you if you sell or refinance the property before a certain date as described in the loan agreements. This allows lenders to count on the interest from your loan as revenue for a certain period of time and gives them a nice fee if you decide to break the agreement to sell or refinance. These fees are acceptable to me from bank loans on long-term deals, as I plan to lock in a good rate and pay down the mortgage over time. For deals with private money, you are most likely going to either sell the property or refinance it once you've completed the renovations and stabilized the property. You should have flexibility for these types of deals, and private money should be treated as a bridge to get you closed and renovated so that you can capitalize on the new value with a sale or refinance. A prepayment penalty takes away that flexibility and should be avoided.

A prepayment penalty governs how long the loan can go, and a guaranteed minimum governs how short the loan can be. The concept of guaranteed minimums is common and very prevalent in other industries like property insurance. The way it works is that if you engage in a loan with a Cash Provider, you guarantee that you will pay the provider at least a certain number of months' interest, even if you pay him or her off sooner than that. I once borrowed $80,000 from a lender to buy a small rental deal. I was able to get another investor to agree to buy it from me as soon as we did the renovations and closed on the sale forty-five days after we purchased it. At a rate of 9 percent, we owed him $900 in interest at closing. He wasn't very happy. It almost wasn't worth the paperwork to him. In some circumstances, I am fine with agreeing to a guaranteed minimum, as I understand that Cash Providers have a certain cost of their time, effort, and attention that needs to be accounted for on short-term deals like this. I would rather pay a guaranteed minimum than loan origination points, so this is something I will offer up in negotiations with lenders who want to make sure they are turning a profit on a short-term deal. If you are going to offer a guaranteed minimum, be careful with how long of a minimum you commit to. When I offer this, I normally agree to two to three months at a maximum.

When discussing things like prepayment penalties and guaranteed minimums with potential Cash Providers, you need to address what's behind them. Most likely, providers want to make sure their money stays at work with you. They don't want to lose the interest income they may be relying on, and they may not want to deal with placing the money into another deal in a few months if you plan to pay them back quickly. Address these concerns by offering up something that may be a win-win. If you have a deep pipeline of deals, you may be willing to guarantee placement of their money into another deal within thirty days if you do pay them back. I've even seen investors offer to make monthly payments to their Cash Providers at a lower interest rate in between deals, just to have the money ready for the next opportunity.

PITFALL NO. 4 | Closing without All the Money You Need to Complete the Deal

Some of the best deals in real estate are on a quick timeline. If you can close quickly, distressed real estate can be purchased at a deep discount. That said, the timeline on distressed real estate deals is so fast, you normally don't get the time you need to do all your due diligence. If you buy these deals, it can be tempting to close on the purchase and figure out construction costs after you own the property. Remember that you are paying the Cash Provider interest while you are still figuring out the deal. If your deal needs a significant amount of work, this can cost you several months of carrying costs to get bids or even to hire an architect or an engineer.

If you buy and figure out costs after ownership, the second problem you will have is finding the next round of money to cover construction. Your Cash Provider that lent to you on the purchase may not be able to support you with a construction loan, forcing you to go out and find another Cash Provider who is willing to go into second position behind the first lender. While you are looking for money, the clock is ticking on the loan you took out to buy the property. Trust me, you will lose a lot of sleep in these circumstances.

I once purchased a dilapidated mixed-use building based solely on dollars per square foot, at a price so low that I figured I could find a way to renovate it and make money. The problem I ran into was that the property needed so much work, I ended up holding it for six months just to get permits approved from the town and complete demolition. I borrowed only enough to buy the property and do a little of the construction work, so in six months we were out of money. We ended up burning more time finding the next round of construction dollars. I estimated that I needed another $100,000 to finish the job but was able to put together only $50,000 at the time. Once I found that capital, we were at least able to get to the next phase of construction, but I soon found more issues with the building and increased our construction costs again. This happened a few more times, and before I knew it, the project timeline had gone well over what it was supposed to and cost me much more than it should have. Had I just gone in and found all the money I needed plus some contingency allowance up front, I could have gotten the job done faster and at a lower interest cost.

The risk to Cash Providers on deals like this is that they are in a deal without a clear exit strategy. The hold time may need to be extended again and again, which increases your interest cost on the deal as well. The risk to both of you is that the deal can go in circles for so long that the money owed to your Cash Providers exceeds the value of the property.

I'm not telling you to avoid distressed properties or fast-closing deals. Sometimes these are the best deals, as other investors will be leery of them for the same reasons, meaning you can get them for a great price. However, I am recommending you tread carefully. Here are a few tips when buying distressed properties that will keep you and your Cash Provider protected:

- **Assume the worst.** Put together an estimate of construction up front and assume the absolute worst-case scenario. If the deal works for that number, you have built in a bit of a safety net. Line up as much potential money as you can. This is money you don't borrow but might borrow if you need it. Cash Providers who have worked with you in the past may be willing to set aside some cash for you that's available on short notice if you ask and offer favorable terms.
- **Have a backup plan.** When buying a distressed deal, you should always have at least two or three options to profit on the deal. Option one could be to renovate and refinance, option two could be to renovate and sell, and option three could be to wholesale the deal right after you buy it if you can't figure out a path with option one or two.
- **Bring some of your cash.** For distressed deals in which the path is not 100 percent clear, you may need to bring in some of your own money to inject

into the deal to keep things moving. If you are a newer investor with limited funds, I recommend that you stay away from these hairy deals until you've built up some cash coffers.

Documents for Setting Up a Private Loan

Now that you've figured out a win-win arrangement and negotiated the terms of your loan, it's time to put together the documents that bind you and the Cash Provider together.

DOCUMENT NO. 1 | Promissory Note

This note is the "I owe you" of the deal. It is where the Deal Providers acknowledge that they owe money to the Cash Providers and give the terms of the loan including interest rate, points, and loan maturity date. Any of the loan terms that are negotiated between the Cash and Deal Providers should be listed in this document, as this is where the loan gets defined. It also says what happens to the loan terms if the loan is not paid back by the maturity date, which is when the loan goes into default. What's interesting is that the promissory note can stand by itself. It doesn't even need to be involved in real estate. These documents are used for unsecured personal and business loans. Anytime money is lent from one party to another, a promissory note is most likely involved.

For real estate transactions, this document doesn't give the lender the right to foreclose on the property or give any collateral aside from the borrower's word that he or she will pay back the Cash Provider. In short, this document is what binds the Deal and Cash Providers together. The original copy of the note is held by the Cash Provider, with a copy going to the Deal Provider. Once the loan is paid back, the promissory note is no longer in effect. For good measure on my deals, I ask my Cash Provider to mail the note to me with *Paid in Full* written at the bottom with their signature. The promissory note by itself just documents the terms of the loan and has both parties agree to those terms. By itself, it's not a document that has any collateral or security, meaning there is nothing that the Cash Provider can take if the loan doesn't get paid back.

DOCUMENT NO. 2 | Mortgage Security Document

The mortgage security document is also called a deed of trust in some states, but it accomplishes the same result. As the promissory note binds the Deal and Cash Providers, this document is what binds the Cash Provider to the real estate collateral. This document creates a lien on the property. A lien is a claim against the property, meaning that the lien holder has some rights that are legally given by the owner of the real estate. Every state in the country has different laws associated with these things, but here are the two rights that lien holders have in general.

- **Lien Holder Right No. 1** – The property owner cannot resell or refinance the property without the lender's permission.
- **Lien Holder Right No. 2** – The lender can begin a foreclosure proceeding if the loan goes into default as defined in the loan terms of the promissory note. The method of foreclosure varies by state, but the result is the same: The owner will lose the real estate in an effort to pay back the lien holders.

This document gives quite a bit of power to the Cash Providers, as they can prohibit the Deal Providers' progress if they choose. Because they have these rights, they have true collateral for their loan.

The mortgage security document itself is what gets filed in the public record once it's signed by the borrower. This is typically done by a title company when the property gets purchased, but in most states, you can walk into the county clerk's office and file it yourself. The methods differ, but, again, the result is the same. The document has to be filed publicly for it to go into effect. It's not like the promissory note, which can just get locked in a safe somewhere. Once the mortgage security document is filed, the lien holder typically gets the original in the mail from the courthouse. When it's time for the property to be paid off, there are specific documents the holder has to sign that vary by state, which removes the lien.

Additional Documents for More Collateral

The promissory note and the mortgage security document are all that's needed for a fully secured real estate loan. As long as the loan terms are clearly defined in the note and the mortgage is properly filed in the public record, the loan is in place. That said, some Cash Providers may want to see additional collateral to further protect their position, especially if they are new to providing loans for real estate deals. Here are two additional documents that sometimes come into play.

ADDITIONAL COLLATERAL DOCUMENT NO. 1 | *Personal Guarantee*
A personal guarantee is an extra step in providing additional collateral to a loan and is the most commonly requested type of collateral by lenders. Al-

most any bank will ask for a personal guarantee on smaller deals, and most hard money lenders ask for this also.

This document is just what it sounds like—it's an instrument that holds the borrower personally liable for the loan. It allows the lender to go after the borrower on a personal level if the loan is not repaid. The borrower's personal assets—including the person's cash and personal assets like his or her home and personal property—become the additional collateral. Those assets are not accessible immediately, and as with a mortgage, the lender will have to commence legal action to take ownership of those assets. If the borrower is set up as an LLC, the lender will most likely ask for someone who is a manager of the company to step in and sign off on a personal guarantee to back the company up.

Some people assume that the promissory note automatically ties the Deal Provider to the loan as a personal guarantor. It doesn't, even if the borrower is an individual, not a company. A personal guarantee is most easily enforced if it's a separate document.

ADDITIONAL COLLATERAL DOCUMENT NO. 2 I *Deed in Lieu of Foreclosure*

Although the mortgage security document gives the lender a lien on the property, the lender has to instigate a foreclosure proceeding to take ownership of the property. This can take three to six months in some states and two to three years in others. The foreclosure process is not immediate, which means that the lender's money will remain tied up in the property during that time and the property will continue to deteriorate if it's in bad condition.

A deed in lieu of foreclosure turns the deed of the property over to the lender if the borrower goes into default on the loan. The lender then takes ownership of the property immediately, without having to wait through a foreclosure process. This is a good thing, but the lender also takes on everything else attached to the property. If the borrower did not pay the real estate taxes, that debt follows the deed. If there are other liens on the property, the lender will have to deal with those lien holders also.

A deed in lieu is a very powerful instrument, and not all borrowers will sign one because it doesn't give the borrower much time to bring the loan back into good standing to avoid losing the property. I have signed deeds in lieu when asked because I believe in my projects and my team to get the deals done. I also will add additional time to the promissory note to extend the grace period leading up to the loan going into default when I'm asked to sign a deed in lieu.

This instrument is not legally enforceable in every state, and I've been asked to sign it in states where it's not. If a lender asks you for this or if you want to offer it up for additional collateral, make sure that your Cash Providers can do something with it if needed.

The Beginning and the End ▮ Two Days That Matter Most

There are two days that matter most on a private loan: the day you close on the purchase and the day you pay off the loan. Let's first talk about the day you close on your purchase.

- If you are just getting started, make sure that you use a title company or an attorney as a third party to ensure that you get all the documents signed and filed properly in the public record. In most states, either of the two can help you with this. They will handle all these things for you, and the good ones will even teach you what they are doing so that you can do some of that work yourself on future deals.

- It may sound obvious, but you need to keep your lenders aware of this day in advance so that they have the money ready. The money may not be sitting in their checking account waiting on your phone call, so give them at least two weeks' notice of closing if you can. For a self-directed IRA loan, they will need at least that much time to get their custodian to release the funds to you.

- Have the Cash Provider send the money to your attorney or title company to hold the money for him or her until closing. I have had the money sent over days in advance just to make sure we can fund the purchase when the closing day comes.

- Make sure the Cash Provider gets a copy of *everything*. The closing statement, the promissory note (the provider gets the original), a copy of the mortgage security document (the original gets sent to the county clerk for filing), and any other docs that are signed at the closing table.

The day you sell or refinance will most likely be the day you pay the loan off, and it's just as important. Here are some thoughts on best practices:

- Just as with the day you buy, you need to keep the lender in the loop on this one. You will need the lender's close cooperation to get to closing and won't be able to sell or refinance without his or her help.

- The first item you will need from the lender is a payoff letter, stating how much you owe. If you deferred all the interest and didn't make monthly payments, the interest you owe will need to be calculated from the day of closing back to the date on the promissory note. If you made monthly payments, you still owe interest calculated from the date of your last payment to the day of closing. The interest you owe is calculated by determining the daily interest due, called a per diem rate, and then applying it to the number of days you owe interest for. The per diem rate equals the interest rate on the loan times the loan amount, divided by 365 days. If your rate is 9 percent on a $100,000 loan, the per diem rate is $100,000 times 9 percent, divided by 365, which equals $24.66 per day. The payoff letter should state the original loan amount plus all the interest due to the day of closing and should also state the per diem rate, just in case closing gets pushed back a day or two unexpectedly.

- The next item you will need is a discharge of mortgage. This is what removes the lender's lien from the property. Different states have different requirements. Most require that this document be notarized. Others go beyond a discharge of mortgage and require that the lender send the original mortgage to the title company or the county clerk so that it can be removed from title. It's important for you to look into how a lien gets properly removed in your state before you do a deal.

- This last suggestion may seem obvious, but it can get overlooked in the hustle and bustle to get to closing. You should reach out to your lender and have a conversation about the deal you are closing and the path forward. Ask lenders for feedback on how you performed as a Deal Provider. Did you meet their expectations? What could you do better on the next deal? What do they want to do with the capital you are sending back to them? It's in these conversations that you can forge a long-term relationship with your Cash Providers and learn to rely on each other as strategic partners.

Final Thoughts on Private Loans

Private loans are the most common types of real estate investments for small- and midsize investors. They are not that complicated and can be a phenomenal vehicle for both sides. I think that, along with all the other benefits, they are best designed as short-term deals. If you can keep them as a quick in-and-out transaction, you can create a pipeline of Cash Providers ready for capital to lend you for your deals.

Also remember the concept of a win-win. The way the Deal Providers win is by having capital available at a predictable cost that's low enough for them to profit as well. The way the Cash Providers win is by having their investment capital constantly at work with plenty of collateral, earning a return that's high enough to compete with other investment options.

I may sound like a broken record, but make sure you consult with an attorney when you create your first couple of loans. As I've outlined in this chapter, each state has its own rules around loans, and you want to make sure your deals are compliant. Additionally, any Cash Provider will see more value in the Deal Provider who has done his or her homework to ensure that the loan documents and the lending process being used are legal in the particular state. Don't leave this research up to your Cash Providers, as they will lose trust in you if it comes out that the way you are structuring your deals is not allowed in their state or takes away some of their collateral.

CHAPTER 8
HOW TO STRUCTURE PRIVATE EQUITY DEALS

Many Deal Providers I speak with never move over to the equity side of investing, at least passive equity. They are more likely to set up a business partnership with another active investor who brings money to the table. Perhaps the Realtor who is a great salesperson partners with a contractor or another investor with lots of Cash Provider contacts. All the owners in a partnership inject some sort of sweat for their ownership and most likely they invest cash as well. There are many reasons that investors may enter into a business partnership and share ownership of deals, but this is not private equity.

Private equity investments are passive for your investors. They may have voting rights and some other benefits associated with owning an LLC and may even be responsible for personally guaranteeing loans. However, they are not active, meaning that they don't handle the day-to-day management of the asset or the property, nor do they inject any sweat equity for their ownership. Their main equity is earned from their cash investment.

These types of investments can seem more complicated to Deal Providers, and many don't want to give away any of their ownership, so they avoid it. Others are afraid of the perceived legal ramifications that come along with equity. We will get into these ramifications later, but I can assure you that in most cases, the downside risk is very similar if not identical to the risk associated with private loans, and the upside is usually better with equity deals for both parties.

Revisiting the BRRRR Strategy

You can go your entire investment career sticking to private loans on your deals without crossing over into providing passive equity investments. I know a few full-time landlords who own several hundred units—with a few employees to help run them—and they own 100 percent of that portfolio. It can be done, over time.

That said, investors who stick to private loans and the BRRRR strategy most likely don't own anything over ten units. The larger buildings they own are typically trade-ups they did with a 1031 exchange, taking the profit from the sale of some smaller assets and trading into one larger building. There is nothing wrong with this, but it takes time and you have to get it right with the BRRRR strategy every time. Additionally, the BRRRR strategy works well on smaller deals like single-family homes and multifamilies under ten units. The reason for this is that a smaller deal has lower risk of a downside. If you do a few BRRRR deals and get left with an unpaid loan balance after refinance, it can stunt your growth, but on a small deal, you will get over it. You may need to write a small check to your lenders if you can't get them out on the refinance or, worst case, cut them in on your next project at a higher rate.

Let's say you buy a duplex for $50,000 in a C class neighborhood. It's not occupied and needs $40,000 to bring it up to your standards and prepare it for your tenants. You borrow the money at 10 percent for six months and are able to line up 100 percent of the purchase and loan amount. Once the property is renovated and leased, you go to refinance out your loan of $90,000, plus interest of $4,500 to get your lender paid back. To your dismay, the property appraises for only $110,000. At 75 percent loan to value, that gives you a new mortgage at $82,500, leaving $12,000 still owed to get your lender out. Ideally, this won't ever happen to you, but if it does, you have some options. You could just write the lender a check for the $12,000 at closing, which could be painful, but if you've done a few deals, you can likely pull this off. You could also pay the lender $1,000 per month plus the continued 10 percent interest on the loan for twelve months, with monthly payments of $1,100. If your lender really needs cash now, you could go out and get a no-interest credit card and take out a cash advance of $12,000 to pay back the loan and then pay off the card out of cash flow. You could also bring your lender into the next deal you do with a commitment to get the lender the $12,000 out of your next deal's equity and/or profit. It's a problem, and the solutions can be a bit painful, but it's not a showstopper. The bottom line is that you do whatever it takes to take care of your investors and protect their money.

On larger deals, all the numbers have more zeros on them. If you were to try to buy, renovate, and refinance an apartment building with little or no equity of your own in the deal, you could end up owing the lender several hundred thousand dollars when it's complete. You can pull off projects like this, and some Deal Providers do it, but you can be sure that they have a backup plan if they can't get all the Cash Provider's loan out of the deal when the refinance comes around.

What if you bought a fifty-unit apartment complex that was in bad shape? It was only 50 percent occupied and needed repairs to lease out the rest of the units and bring it up to a healthy status all around. The price you were able to negotiate on the building was $1,500,000, and you estimated repairs to be $500,000, bringing your total capital required to $2,000,000. You really like this deal and want to keep it for yourself, and you have a deep network of Cash Provider lenders, so you borrow all or most of the capital from them. You could go to bank on this, but the bank is not going to be OK with those other lenders putting a lien on the property also. You have to go with 100 percent private loans on this one. Say it takes you a year to get the renovations done, as it's a larger deal, and at 10 percent interest, you owe an additional $200,000 to your lenders. Once you complete the renovations, you find that the value you added brought the value of the complex up to $2,400,000, which is a nice bump in value. Even with that large increase in value of the building, you would still be underwater if you went with a private loan structure on this deal. At 75 percent loan to value, your new mortgage will be $1,800,000, meaning you still owe your lenders an additional $400,000. There are larger deals in which a loan strategy may work, but you could be left owing quite a bit if things don't go as planned.

Before I move on, I want to be clear about something here. I am not saying that private loans, the BRRRR strategy, and buying smaller deals are a bad way to go. As I said earlier, I recommend that most investors start with that path and grow into larger deals and equity. There are a few gurus out there who will tell new investors to go big or go home when they start their investing career. I don't agree with this and think that investors should grow as they go, stretching themselves slightly every time they do a deal.

Reasons That Deal Providers Should Consider Equity

It can be tempting to keep all the ownership to yourself. In my experience, there are three reasons that you should consider doing deals with equity:

Private Equity Reason No. 1

Remember the example I gave with the BRRRR strategy going south on a large deal? Well, what if instead of borrowing all that money from a lender, you get a mortgage from a bank to cover 50 percent of the purchase price? Since the property is 50 percent occupied, you will most likely be able to qualify for this size of a loan based on the property's income. You raise the rest of the money you need from a group of investors who put up the remainder of the purchase price (or $750,000) and the renovations of $500,000, and you raise an additional $150,000 as a cash reserve, so $1,400,000 in total investment from your Cash Providers. After renovations, your new value is $2,400,000, allowing a new mortgage for $1,800,000 at 75 percent loan to value. You pay off the first mortgage of $750,000 and now have an additional $1,050,000 in cash from the refinance to pay back your investors some of their capital. In most cases, your investors retain their percentage of ownership of the deal, but since you are giving them their money back, they now have some or all of their investment capital returned to go into your next project. More on how to structure this later.

Private Equity Reason No. 2

Because private equity provides a vehicle to bring money into a deal alongside a bank loan, it creates the opportunity to do larger deals. Unless you have $500,000 of your own to put into a project, you are left doing deals you can afford to do with your own money or deals that make sense with the BRRRR strategy. Additionally, offering some ownership of deals can sweeten the pot enough to attract larger investors to your projects. For some of my larger fix-and-flips, we have offered a piece of the profit to lenders who are willing to fund the whole project.

Private Equity Reason No. 3

As you know, projects don't always go as planned. Putting together equity deals gives you a hedge just in case. Let me explain. Construction costs can go way over budget, or the market can shift while you are renovating your property. Any number of things can happen. As much as it may be tempting to try to take down a larger deal with all private loans and hope for the best, you could end up with a loss that could put you out of the business for good. Giving away some of the ownership to investors will help you structure your deal differently so that you are not committed to paying a certain interest rate on their money; you pay them a percentage of the profit. If the deal doesn't make as much as you projected, your investors will most likely make most of the profit, but at least you won't owe them money when the deal is done. You won't make as much as you would on the upside, but you won't lose either. Let me be clear: There are ways to protect you and the investor in circumstances like this because I don't want you to confuse what I'm saying with getting your investors to bear the loss instead of you.

While I know some investors who have a few hundred units that they own all by themselves, I don't know *any* investors who have more than a thousand units who don't have equity investors in the deals with them. If you choose to do deals with private loans only, you can build a solid small- to medium-sized portfolio for yourself, but you will hit a ceiling on the size of deal you can do. Equity takes away the glass ceiling of real estate investing and opens up possibilities to do deals much larger than private loans will allow.

Now that we've established why you may want to consider using equity on your deals, let's talk more about how to select the right Cash Provider, deal, and structure and the documents you need to have in place to set things up and, most important, protect everyone involved.

Which Cash Providers Are Right for Equity Deals?

When you start talking to more and more Cash Providers, you will encounter many who are savvier and know the perceived profit potential from real estate investments, and they will want to get into the ownership side of your deals. Although the prospective returns on equity deals may seem attractive and temp almost any investor to jump in, only some will actually want to deal with the risks associated with equity deals. It's important for all Deal Providers to talk about the risks that come along with these types of deals so that your investor is informed, and for larger deals, disclosing these risks is required by the SEC. I went over the risks of equity deals briefly in a previous chapter, but I want to outline these risks again from the perspective of how they will automatically exclude some investors.

- **RISK NO. 1 I *Illiquidity*.** Equity investments are considered to be illiquid, meaning they can't be easily converted to cash. Cash Providers' shares may produce nice dividend checks for them, but they most likely can't sell those shares to get their investment back very easily. You need to ask potential Cash Providers directly whether there is any reason they foresee needing the cash they are investing with you back. If you are putting them into a deal with a three-year projection and they need that capital for their kid's college tuition in year three, you may want to find a different investment vehicle for them.

- **RISK NO. 2 | *Banks.*** When you are doing a deal requiring bank financing, your lender will want to review your company formation documents to determine who the owners are and who should be guaranteeing the loan. Not all loans require a personal guarantee, but all will require owners who have a majority interest or management responsibilities to agree to the loan and to provide a personal guarantee if required. Most banks view any owner with more than 25 percent interest in a company a majority interest owner. If you have a Cash Provider who is putting a significant amount of money into your deal, you will need to inform the person about showing up on the bank's radar. If it's a concern to your Cash Provider, there are ways around the personal guarantee requirement, and you should talk to your lender and attorney up front about ways around this. Although there are workarounds, you need to be up front with the Cash Providers about your disclosure requirements with your bank. If they are not OK with this, equity may not be the right fit for them.

- **RISK NO. 3 | *Time.*** Your Cash Providers should view their investments in equity deals as cash they won't get back for a very long time, typically when the property sells, which is dependent on the market and out of your control. This is especially true on rental deals. Although your projections may say that you will get them out in five years, that may turn into seven years, or it could be three years. Your role as a Deal Provider on an equity transaction is to make your investors the best return you can, which may require them to keep their money in your deal for longer than anticipated.

- **RISK NO. 4 | *Ups and Downs.*** Most savvy investors will tell you that they want to get into equity deals with you because they see the potential returns they can make if the deal goes better than expected. If the fix-and-flip they own part of sells for 10 percent more, they get a chunk of that increase. If you raise rents by $100 per month on a property, some of that increase is theirs. It's easy for them to see that side of it, but you also need to let them know that just as they are tied to the profit increase, they are part owner if the deal doesn't meet projections as well. If the fix-and-flip sells for below target, they don't make as much of a return. If a tenant moves out and trashes the unit, which takes a few months of vacancy to repair and turn around, the investors may not receive their typical dividend check that month. They may even need to put in additional cash to keep the deal moving, which is known as a cash call. Equity investors need to be OK with the volatility of the investment. The returns aren't fixed as they are in a loan, so if your Cash Provider can't handle the ups and downs that come with these investments, they may be more comfortable in something that provides a fixed stream of income.

- **RISK NO. 5 | *Taxes*.** Aside from investing with a self-directed IRA, almost any real estate investment has immediate tax implications to your Cash Providers. As we've already covered, SDIRA owners don't pay tax on their gains until they take them out of their IRA. Other investors will have to pay tax on their gains. The profit on the fix-and-flip or the rental income gain becomes taxable to them right away. Although rental income has its tax advantages, Cash Providers need to be educated enough to set aside some of their profits to pay the IRS on their gains if need be. You are not their tax advisor and don't want to pose as such, but you do need to give them the heads-up to talk to their CPA about their work with you so that they can be prepared for a tax bill if one is coming.

If there are specific risks associated with the deal you are doing, make sure to disclose them also. As you do more complex deals and get into syndications, disclosure of risks becomes very important. It will also help you build long-term trust with your Cash Providers if you are clear with them that you are looking out for their best interests by letting them know of the risks associated with the deal.

Equity Investment Vehicles

Now that we've talked about how to determine whether a Cash Provider is right for an equity deal by reviewing the risks reviewing the risks with him or her, let's get into what you can offer to help the provider reach his or her goals.

Turnkey Rentals

A turnkey deal is one in which the Deal Provider finds a rental property, repairs it, fills it with good tenants, and sells it to another investor. The Deal Provider will typically agree to manage the property for the investor or has a strategic alliance with a local property manager. The Cash Provider is the buyer of the property, and the deliverable the Deal Provider is giving is a hands-off rental property.

Some of you may not view a turnkey as an equity deal, but it is. You are providing ownership to the Cash Providers; you are giving them 100 percent ownership. Although they are not investing alongside you in the deal, they are trusting you to deliver a reliable product to them. If you can do this, they will invest in these deals again and again with you.

These deals are perfect for the Cash Provider who wants a good return, can afford to weather the storm if a tenant moves out, and wants the control that comes with owning the property outright. Cash Providers can leverage their return further by putting debt on the property with a mortgage, which they obtain on their own. They can also own it free and clear if they have the cash for that. If they want to fire the property manager or manage it themselves, they can do that as well. If they want to sell, they can. Some Cash Providers really like these deals, as they can get into them with not much money, especially if they use some debt. It's not a complete hands-off investment, as the Cash Providers will most likely need to pay some of the bills themselves, like the mortgage, insurance, and taxes. They will also have to spend a bit of time checking on the property manager's effectiveness each month and may even go to walk the properties every now and then to confirm they are in good condition. These are typical activities of an owner. They are actions the Deal Provider would perform if they had some ownership of the property, but since they don't, it's up to the Cash Provider. In exchange for control, Cash Providers may be willing to go this route for their investments. In a nutshell, I recommend turnkeys to high-paid professionals who want to invest full-time eventually. They can qualify for a mortgage, and they understand the importance of not spending everything they earn, which will allow them to set aside enough to buy a few turnkeys a year from a Deal Provider they trust.

On the other side, turnkeys are a win for a Deal Provider who is set up to handle them. As I said in a previous chapter, a turnkey is a fix-and-flip and BRRRR hybrid. You still buy, renovate, and rent the property, but instead of the third R (refinance), you sell the property to a Cash Provider. What's great is that if you deliver a good product and pick a Cash Provider with some capacity, you can line yourself up to do multiple deals a year with the same buyer.

I think turnkeys are a good vehicle for Deal Providers who are established in a certain investment area. This happened to us a few years ago. We have been doing business in Trenton for many years and have gotten to know many of the wholesalers and Realtors in an area. I was already active with the local REIA club, which helped generate leads as well. As we grew our business into larger projects, I faced a dilemma: I had grown into larger projects but was still getting leads for good deals on single-family homes and small multifamilies. On the other side, I had investors who wanted to get into investing and, for many of the reasons I've already listed, were a good fit for turnkey deals. These turnkey deals allow us to maintain our local relationships for leads while helping Cash Providers who want turnkeys to build their portfolios. And since we are the ones selling the deals, we make a chunk of cash, which I am able to put into a larger project. We do only a few of these deals a year, but there are companies that have built a whole business around this strategy and do hundreds of closings a year with buyers from all around the world.

These deals are pretty straightforward to execute. Once you have your systems and necessary licenses in place for management and construction, you just need to find a deal that you can buy at the right price. You can follow this plan of attack to structure your deals:

- Find Cash Providers who are looking for a turnkey. Make sure they can obtain a loan from a bank if needed. Get clear on what their desired return on investment is and show them a hypothetical situation for a turnkey with a reasonable management fee included. I try to calculate what price per door works, considering average expenses and market rents in the target area. If you are on the same page on the price per door for deals, you can move forward to the next step. Let's say for this conversation, you agree that a sell price of around $60,000 per door for a rental is good, as long as it's leased for $800 per unit per month on average.

- Given your market and your team, you should know roughly what it will cost to make a bank-owned dilapidated property a solid rentable property. This should include as many upgrades as you can afford to make to provide a reliable and easily leasable product. In my market, I can replace a kitchen, heating system, bathroom, flooring, and paint for around $20,000 per unit. For a small multi, I can probably get a new roof on the property for that number as well.

- Once you know your sell price target and your average cost to renovate, you just need to find a deal that works. I try to target a profit margin of 20 percent of the sell price of my fix-and-flips and turnkey deals as a benchmark. If you throw in another 5 percent for buying and selling closing costs, plus 5 percent for carrying costs, that puts me at a target buy price for a turnkey of $60,000 times 70 percent, which equals $42,000, minus $20,000 in construction, or $22,000 per unit. It's not easy to find that deal, and sometimes I have to tweak my construction or completed sell price to make it work.

- Once I find a deal, I will lock it up under agreement and then go to my Cash Providers and get them to commit to it up front, thereby guaranteeing my sale. They will start working on getting approval from their lender and getting their cash together while I finish the property for them.
- I will typically go to a different Cash Provider as a lender to fund the closing and construction. I use a Cash Provider who prefers private loan deals, perhaps with an SDIRA. The Cash Provider is very happy with the collateral on the deal because I can show him or her that I already have a committed buyer on the property.
- During construction, I am offering the property for lease to generate strong interest in the units as soon as they are completed. My goal is to get them occupied as soon as the work is completed and the local town has issued a certificate of occupancy. If you manage in house, this is can be done easily. If you plan on using a third-party manager, you need to get him or her lined up to show the vacant units and commit to managing it when you are done.
- I will look to time closing on the sale immediately after the property is leased, which is a bit of a balancing act with the buyer's lender and appraiser and inspectors. Lenders will want to see my scope of work for repairs because they will see how much less I paid for the property versus the sell price. They want to make sure I added value during the renovations. They will also want copies of the leases with the new tenants.
- The reason I go through all of this is that it compresses the selling time. I can complete a fix-and-flip in six months, and sometimes it takes longer. For a turnkey deal, I can go from purchase to sale as fast as three months, and as long as I can keep construction costs predictable, I know what my profit will be going in because I already know my sell price.

Not everyone has or wants to build a business around this strategy. Some Deal Providers I talk to don't even offer this up as a strategy. Maybe they don't have a construction team they can stand behind to deliver a reliable rental product. Some of my investor friends who do have management and construction contacts look at this model and think that people like me are crazy for going through all that work to renovate and lease out a good deal just to go and sell it when it's done!

These deals are not for everyone, but for those who choose to get into them, they can be lucrative. For this strategy to work as a Deal Provider, you need to establish yourself in a specific regional market so you get leads on deals and also build your Cash Provider group that wants to get into those markets. You also need to have management and construction teams you can rely on that will deliver and maintain a product you can stand behind to your buyers. If you can arrange the systems and find willing buyers, turnkeys can be a good source of income for you and also a desirable investment vehicle for certain Cash Providers.

Joint Venture

By definition, a joint venture is a combination of resources of two or more entities to complete a specific real estate project. The resources of both sides can be any number of things. As I said earlier, I have done joint venture deals with contractors and also with Cash Providers. Most commonly, a joint venture is between a Cash Provider and a Deal Provider and can be viewed as a hybrid of a debt and equity deal. The Cash Provider gets an interest rate on his or her money but also has a claim to the net profits of the project. These can be win-win arrangements and allow you to get into larger and more complex flip projects if you set them up correctly.

The main thing that needs to be defined up front is how the net profit gets calculated. You may think that it's as simple as the sell price minus expenses, but other factors come into play. Some Deal Providers will charge a fee for managing the deal during construction, which is called a developer's fee or a construction management fee. If you plan on charging this, make sure it's disclosed and considered part of the expenses. Other factors like sales commissions and the interest due to the Cash Provider should be deducted before calculating the net profit. Come up with a clear definition of what the net profit is and how it is calculated, and put that definition in the formation documents so everyone is on the same page.

There are a few ways to structure this depending on how much of the Cash Provider's money you are borrowing for your project. Although these deals sound complex, the structure is pretty straightforward. It really comes down to whether or not you are using bank financing on these deals. If you aren't using bank financing and the Cash Providers are giving you most or all of the purchase and construction costs, you can simply reference their stake to a percentage of profit in the promissory note. To be clear, you are not giving them ownership of the property; you are just pledging a percent of your net proceeds. Make sure you are clear about that with the Cash Providers. Instead of ownership, they have a lien on the property via a mortgage and a note, which gives them a return on their money plus a chunk of the net profit.

If you are using a mortgage from a bank on your deal, your lender may not want to see subsequent mortgages coming in from your Cash Providers behind it. Unless your lender is very flexible and accepts other mortgages, you will need to use another method to protect your Cash Provider. We've accomplished this by having our attorney draft a simple joint venture agreement. The agreement defines what we bring to the table (which is the deal), the mortgage from the bank personally guaranteed by us, the management of the renovations, and the supervision of the sales process. It also defines what the Cash Providers bring, which is their cash. It defines their share of the net profit and how that's calculated and the rate of return they get on their money along with the profit. This document does not give the Cash Providers collateral as a mortgage security document does, so there is more perceived risk. It also allows your Cash Providers to operate behind the scenes, as they don't go on the title of the property as an owner.

If they are looking for more collateral, you can accomplish this by setting up a new LLC that takes ownership of the property and gives them ownership of that company directly. I am not a fan of this method, as it requires you to set up an LLC for every deal you do, and it may require you to disclose your Cash Providers to the bank, which may be a problem for them.

We recently came across a deal to build three townhomes in Philadelphia. The cost of the land was $210,000, with construction slated to cost $650,000. The sell price of the homes when completed would yield us $375,000 per house after real estate commission, conservatively. It was a good deal all around. I didn't want to borrow all the money from a private lender because I was concerned about the carrying costs. Paying $210,000 for the land and $650,000 for construction added up to a loan of $860,000, which would cost me $6,450 per month at 9 percent interest! No thanks. I had a bank that would fund the majority of the construction costs if I could buy the land with equity. The bank's interest rate on the construction loan was much more attractive at 5 percent, or $2,708 per month. On top of that, it would lend me $25,000 as an interest reserve, which would cover the monthly payment for nine months. I just needed to find the capital for the land and some equity to fund the first round of construction. I had an investor with a sizable SDIRA who wanted to work with me. I showed him this deal, and he expressed strong interest. After a review of a joint venture agreement by his attorney, we struck a deal for him to put $290,000 into the project at an interest rate of 8 percent, plus 10 percent of the profit on the deal. His money would cost me $1,400 per month, for a total interest cost of $4,108. Although I had to give up 10 percent of our profit on the deal,

I was more than happy to do that to get access to much cheaper financing from my bank for the majority of the project costs. The Cash Provider was willing to do the deal because it gave him access to the upside on the sale of the property, increasing his return to well over 14 percent annually.

Rental Properties

Owning rentals long term with Cash Providers may be what most people think of when talking about equity investors in real estate. Although it's the most common arrangement, it's not the only way to do rental deals, as I hope to have shown you by this point. From midsize apartment buildings to office complexes to shopping malls, medium- and large-sized rental deals get done with some form of arrangement with passive investors. I also can tell you firsthand that it's not only medium- and large-sized deals that can get done this way. I got started doing small rental deals with investors until I learned the ropes and grew into larger deals. I break rental deals with equity investors into two categories:

Small Rental Deals

A good way to get started in equity is on smaller deals. This is how I got started. I was able to find a couple investors who were willing to invest their cash if I was willing to be the legs. They did have a role and a voting interest in the company, even if it was a small one. They had to personally guarantee loans when the company we formed needed to borrow money. Although they didn't have a day-to-day role as I did in the company, they had the same rights, making them equal partners with me. Since there are only one or two partners on this type of deal, the deal size is typically smaller, perhaps consisting of only a few single-family homes or a small multifamily.

I like these deal arrangements because they allow you to start on a smaller project with a key investor who may want a little more control and is willing to show up on bank loans. This investor could be a good one to build a relationship with to help you grow into larger projects.

Syndication

A syndication is a collective of a larger group of investors. These investors are typically passive, meaning they don't have any roles or responsibilities in the company. Because they have a smaller ownership stake and no management responsibilities, they normally don't have to personally guarantee any loans taken on by the company. These deals normally involve larger properties and groups of investors. They require compliance with the SEC because they involve the purchase of a security. Syndications should not be your first, second, or third deal in this business, but they can be something to aspire to. They give you access to larger projects and are a good investment vehicle for your Cash Providers once you've established a solid database of investors and have a track record of successful deals behind you.

These deals can be focused on one large purchase or a few smaller ones. My first true syndication was with four investors who put in $300,000 total. We purchased several small rental deals, renovated them and refinanced, and then repeated. Because I was the only manager, I was the only one required to personally guarantee the loans. We started on a few small four-family deals but were able to roll the capital over a few times. That company now owns nineteen units of rentals and invested in a condo project as a passive investor as well.

Setting Up the Equity Structure

Setting up your first equity deal can be scary. There are certain documents and entity setup steps you need to know very well that will help you structure these deals in a manner that protects you and your investors. These documents and entity setup can also serve as a means to document all the terms of the agreements you have with your Cash Providers and even offer incentives to you for producing a solid return for them.

Limited Liability Company

Although there are other entities out there, including limited partnerships, S corporations, C corporations, and land trusts, the most common entity used in real estate is the LLC. It can be set up easily—in most states, you can set one up yourself on the state's website. They are pass-through entities for gains and losses, meaning they don't pay tax themselves. Instead, all the gain or loss gets passed directly to the underlying owners. This provides a huge benefit to owners of investment real estate through an LLC because of depreciation. As we reviewed earlier, depreciation is a paper loss that owners of rental real estate get to take each year as a claim against their income on the property. Because LLCs are pass-through entities, owners get to take that loss directly on their personal tax return. This is a double-edged sword, as the same rules apply to gains. If the LLC performs a fix-and-flip or sells a rental, the income from that sale goes right to the personal tax returns of the owners, requiring them to claim that gain as a capital gain.

LLCs also give owners some anonymity from the public. You and your investors' personal names and home addresses are not shown on the public record as the owners of the property. The LLC and its address are shown. Although in most states you can figure out who is behind the LLC, it's challenging to get that information. I have friends who own investment properties that they manage themselves but own through an LLC. They self-manage, so they do their own showings and take the maintenance calls. They never tell the tenants that they own the property; they introduce themselves as the "property manager." If they have to deliver bad news like a rent increase, they can blame it on the "owner." If the tenant has a request, they can say, "Let me ask the owner," to separate themselves a bit from the decision if it's not favorable. I've never used this tactic myself, but LLCs allow owners to be anonymous, which can be a help at times.

There are many derivations of LLCs out there, but the ones I want to highlight for you here are the *member managed* and *manager managed*. A member managed company gives control of the company to all members. These companies are common for partnerships where all the owners have an active role in the company. If there is a dispute on actions the company needs to take, there are parameters in the operating agreement on how to resolve them, which is typically by a vote where the majority wins. Each member is typically empowered to sign for the company on documents and otherwise act on the company's behalf in all ways.

A manager managed LLC has an appointed manager or managers of the company. Those managing members are empowered to perform the duties of the company on all matters. The managers are compensated, typically with ownership and sometimes a fee for their roles. The managers are empowered to make decisions that best benefit the rest of the members in all the company's affairs. There are also members of the company who have ownership but limited or no roles in the day-to-day activities of the business. These are the passive investors, who most likely provided the seed capital for the LLC when it started up. Although they don't have day-to-day control, they typically can vote to remove the manager if they can prove that the manager is no longer acting in their best interest.

A similar entity to a manager managed LLC is a limited partnership. In this structure, there is a general partner, who plays a similar role to that of the managing member, and limited partners, who are the members. I've used both of them in deal formations and have found that banks and attorneys tend to view them interchangeably.

Both of these formations for LLCs are beneficial in real estate transactions. The manager managed LLC is most likely the way you will go if you are forming a strategic partnership with another investor or entity that will be an active partner in some fashion in the business. For my first couple of equity deals, I went with member managed LLCs because I needed my partners to provide a personal guarantee on the loans, and since I had a shorter track record, they wanted more control of the company. As our track record for these types of deals grew, I have grown to using manager managed LLCs, in which our investors step into the passive member role and my company sits as the manager.

Setting Up the LLC with the State and the Fed

For those of you who have never set up an LLC before, I am going to go over the steps you need to take to get it done. Although attorneys are necessary in setting these entities up, I have found that you can do the state and federal filings on your own and bring the attorney in to help with the operating agreement.

LLCs are first created at the state level, typically by going to the state's website and filling out some forms there. This is where the name, address, and registered agent for the company are established. The company can have an address outside the state of incorporation, as well, but needs to have a registered agent with an in-state address. You can serve in this role yourself or use several companies out there that will serve in this role for you at a reasonable fee. I typically set up my LLCs in the state in which they will do most of their business. If I'm buying a building in North Carolina, that will be the state of incorporation of the LLC. I know that there are states with greater benefits, and I've heard of investors using Nevada- and Delaware-based LLCs because of the benefits that arise both from a tax and an anonymity perspective. I've never bothered with this because it seems more complicated than it's worth, but you should look into the benefits of incorporating in different states and make a decision that suits your needs and goals.

Then you go to the IRS website and get an employer identification number (EIN) for your LLC. Don't get thrown off by the name, as you don't need to have employees to have an EIN. The EIN for the IRS and the federal government is used to track your company's business. It's also called a federal tax ID number, which is similar to a Social Security number for an individual. You also use this number to set up a bank account for the LLC, and it is how the IRS will trace revenue you make back to you for tax purposes. These two actions to set up an LLC with the government are only half of the process. The next step is much more important, which is setting up the entity between its partners with an operating agreement.

The Operating Agreement

LLCs, and most other entities for that matter, are created by an operating agreement. It can be a lengthy document, as it outlines everything about the company. I've said it perhaps a few hundred times in this book, and I'll say it again here—if you are creating an LLC, you need an attorney to help you with your operating agreement. This document covers all the facets of your business, and it's not worth avoiding the thousand dollars or so that it will cost you to get it written properly and cover all your bases.

Here are the main items you want to make sure get addressed in plenty of detail:

- **The basics** – Name, address, and state of incorporation
- **Purpose of business** – You may also need to file this with the state. Most likely, this will be something like "real estate investment," but if there is a specific property the company will be buying, name it.
- **Managing members** – Who they are, what their roles are, how they are compensated, how they can be removed if necessary, and what their limits of responsibilities are
- **Members** – Their roles, if any, and how much of the company ownership they have. You notice I didn't say "who they are." In most cases, the member investors' information is not in this document, which is a benefit to them. If you use a separate document called a *subscription agreement*, they may not need to disclose their information in the operating agreement. A subscription agreement is what gives your Cash Providers ownership of the company, discloses their qualifications to invest with you, and ties them to the operating agreement.
- **Member exit** – One of the biggest Cash Provider questions is "How long will you have my money, and when will I get it back?" Cash Providers may also want to know how they can get their money back sooner than the end of the project. Although it should have been made clear to them by this point that these investments are not liquid, they will want an out to get their cash back if needed. The way you can accomplish this is by giving them the right to sell their shares internally, to the manager and the members. The price gets negotiated between the buyer and the seller. You can also give them

the right to sell their shares to a third party outside the company, but you may want to give the internal members of the company the right to match the bid that the seller gets from that third party before the sale is allowed.

- **Distributions** – The operating agreement should outline clearly the manager's responsibility to distribute company profits to members. This is one of those things I tend to keep at the manager's discretion because pushing out too much profit can hurt the company if there are expected upcoming expenses. This is part of the manager's role in acting in the investors' best interest. Paying them as much as you can may not be in their long-term interest if it means hindering the company's long-term solvency.·

- **Cash calls** – A cash call is an instance in which the manager goes to the membership and asks for additional investment to accomplish the company's goals. This is usually done when unexpected circumstances arise and the company's cash reserves become depleted to the point that the regular expenses cannot be met. It can also occur if an opportunity arises that is outside the original scope of the money raised but is in line with the mission and goals of the company. Either way, the company needs money to accomplish its goals. The operating agreement needs to specifically outline how the manager approaches the other members to fund this cash requirement.

- **Dispute resolution** – I hope all your deals go extremely smooth. There is a good chance that they will. However, your operating agreement needs to cover all the bases and should outline what you do if you get into a dispute with another manager or a member and can't reach a resolution on your own.

- **Dissolution** – The operating agreement needs to address the dissolution of the company when that time comes as well. This can be as simple as selling all the assets and dividing up the company's cash accordingly, but it will most likely be more complicated than that. It may seem like a long way off, but defining how things get dissolved is important to address when forming the company.

In most instances, the operating agreement gets lots of attention when you first set the company up and then sits on the shelf until you need to reference it. For that reason, some investors don't give it too much attention. If things go as planned in their company, they may get away with this. However, if an unexpected matter arises, like a dispute or a cash call, they will need to rely on the operating agreement. Additionally, you will most certainly need to reference that agreement when it comes time for dissolution.

Preferred Returns

I've mentioned preferred returns a few times in this book. When investors put an equity investment into your deal, the amount of money they put in is called their capital account. A preferred return is a payment that's due to your investors as a percentage of their capital account. They get this return after all expenses are paid but before any profits are distributed, including the manager's side of profits. In essence, if the deal is making money, they are the first to get paid. The preferred return acts as the minimum profit investors will get on their money. They also get a percentage of profit on top of this return, based on their percentage of ownership of the deal.

Here's where this gets more interesting. They get a preferred return based on their capital account, meaning how much money they have in the deal. If you are able to return part of their capital, the preferred return goes down. Perhaps you are able to refinance the property to get some capital to return to them, or maybe some of the profit you pay them goes toward reimbursing their capital accounts. It's important to note that giving them their capital back is only reducing their capital account; it doesn't change their percent of ownership automatically, unless it's defined that way in the operating agreement. If you can find a way to get your investors some or all of their money back, you will reduce or eliminate your obligation to pay a preferred return while they maintain some ownership of the company. It also gives them their seed capital back so they can invest in your next deal if they are happy.

Internal Rate of Return

Many people think about the return that you and your investors get on a property in terms of cash flow, cash-on-cash return, or ROI. These are all valid factors, but the one that very few new investors speak of but need to learn is the IRR, or internal rate of return. The IRR calculation factors in:

- **Annual cash flow** – This needs to include their preferred return (if you are offering one) and their share of the cash flow.
- **Mortgage principal reduction** – If your loan is amortized, your monthly payment will include a contribution to interest and a portion that pays down the amount you owe to the bank. This can be a smaller number on small deals, but on larger rentals, this can be significant and plays a big factor in calculating the profit return.
- **Increase in property value** – This may be harder to figure out on a month-by-month basis if your deal is on the smaller side, but on larger projects,

you can use the monthly profit to calculate the property value through the use of a cap rate. Your property value equals the net operating income (NOI) divided by the cap rate. Each market has a cap rate that's appropriate to use for your type of rental. If you don't know what it is in your area, ask a few commercial real estate agents or an appraiser. The NOI equals your rental income, including vacancy, minus all expenses (not including your mortgage payment).

If your cap rate is 8 percent and your NOI is $100,000 per year, then value = $100,000 / 8 percent = $1,250,000.

If you are able to find a way to increase your annual NOI by $5,000 by raising rents or decreasing expenses, you've added $5,000 divided by 8 percent, or $62,500 in value. Once you know your cap rate, you can track your property value on a monthly basis.

- **Initial investment capital** – This is pretty straightforward, but it should be noted that if you return a portion of the investors' capital at some point in the deal, this will increase their IRR.

The IRR factors in all the ways that the investment increases the net worth of its shareholders. Conversations around the IRR can get complicated, and it involves a relationship between it and the net present value of the investment. In layman's terms, the net present value is the current value of all the future cash flow the investor will make compared with the amount they are investing. Don't get too techy with your investors unless they want to get into that level of financial evaluation. That said, most investors will want to look at the total return they are projected to get when they invest in your deal, so be sure to use a good accounting tool to calculate it for your equity projects.

Determining Your Share

There is a bit of an art when it comes to calculating how much of a deal to give to your investors and how much you want to keep for yourself. I find it helpful to approach this from their perspective and give them a return I know they will be comfortable with, leaving the rest for myself.

When you think about it, a return on an investor's money should consider two factors. The first is some growth rate investors want to see that outperforms the rate of inflation so that they are building their wealth compared with the annual increase in the cost of living. The second factor is a compensation for the risk they are taking in the investment. If the perceived risks are higher and you can't balance out those risks with collateral or other safety nets, you will need to pay them a higher rate of return in exchange for taking that risk.

When you are calculating the investor IRR, take the whole picture into account. How long is their money tied up in the deal? What are the risks that you can't address with collateral? Are you going to return any capital during the project? What are the best- and worst-case scenarios? It also helps to run a deal by a Cash Provider you've been working with for a while, as he or she can give you feedback on how attractive things look at the split levels you are considering.

Other Ways to Sweeten the Pot for Your Cash Providers

Your deal may speak for itself and provide plenty of cash flow to your investors. If so, you may not need to offer additional incentives to them to attract the money you need to get the deal done. If your deal is low cash flow up front or is a larger project, you may need to offer additional incentives. Here are a few to consider. I haven't had to offer either of these to date, but I know those who have used them with success.

- **Waterfalls** – A waterfall structure is a setup where the Deal Provider's ownership and share of the profit is on a sliding scale. At first, it's very low and it may be zero, and it increases as benchmarks for Cash Provider profits are met. This structure is common in deals that require a bunch of stabilization to the target property up front, but once that work is complete, it will cash-flow nicely. The Deal Provider may have to work hard to get the deal performing and will be rewarded with a larger percentage of ownership once the profit targets are achieved. If you are able to hold off on your profit payments for a while, waterfalls can be a win for both sides.
- **Preferred equity** – Perhaps you are doing a deal that is a new construction project or a major renovation of an existing building. You can get financing from a bank for part of the project and can raise the rest from equity investors, but you want to find a way to get more ownership for yourself when the property is complete. You could use a waterfall structure, but those investors are still in the deal with you even at less ownership. Preferred equity is another option that allows you to get investors completely out of the deal once you hit a specific return on investment to them and give them all their capital back. If they are looking for 15 percent per year on their money, you may be able to achieve that number when you finish the property and refinance it. The problem with preferred equity is that it can get expensive if you can't get that investor out when scheduled.

Creative Ways for the Deal Provider to Make Money

Aside from the carve-out ownership that the Deal Provider gets, there are a few other ways that he or she can make additional money on the deal.

- **Acquisition fee** – This is a "success fee" that gets paid to the Deal Provider once the sale closes. It's typically a percentage of the purchase price—between 1 and 3 percent is typical. The intention of the acquisition fee is to compensate the Deal Provider for finding and closing the opportunity. If a personal guarantee or sponsorship is required by the lender, that should be factored into the acquisition fee also.

- **Asset management fee** – There are two schools of thought on this one. One is to view the Deal Provider as a manager of the Cash Provider's asset, his or her cash. It functions like the preferred return mentioned above, only payable to the Deal Provider. The fee is paid as a percentage of the Cash Provider's cash that remains in the deal. If the property gets refinanced and all the Cash Provider's money is returned, the asset management fee goes to zero. The other way to structure the asset management fee is as a percentage of rents collected at the property. The more rent is increased and collections decreased, the more money the Deal Provider makes. This ties the Deal Provider to the success of the property and functions similar to a property management fee. A property management fee can also be charged by the Deal Provider if he or she is self-managing, or it can be a third-party management company that reports to the asset manager.

- **Transaction fee** – This is a fee that gets charged when all the Cash Provider's money is returned to him or her, either from a refinance of the property or from a sale. It's a success fee for giving the initial investment back to your investors, which is a big success point for your Cash Providers. As long as it's reasonable, between 1 and 2 percent of the profit, most investors will agree to it.

A mistake a Deal Provider can make is to "over-fee" a deal. No savvy investor will want to get on board with you if your deal has too many fees that suck too much of the profit out. Investors want to see a win-win, where the more money they make, the more you make. Most are happy to compensate you for finding and managing the deal, as long as that compensation is fair.

Building a Team

Who says the managing member should be only one person? Most successful equity Deal Providers have a small team they work with that helps them with every deal. That team may help find the new opportunities, underwrite the deals, present to investors, or assist with the day-to-day operations once the property is up and running. I've had larger investors mentor me on my deals in exchange for some ownership, and I've done the same for others. As long as anyone receiving a share of the manager's equity plays an active and ongoing role in the project, he or she is treated as part of the management team and can be given ownership by the manager. I should be clear that, as I understand it, you cannot compensate someone with equity strictly for helping you raise money during the funding phase. To earn his or her equity, a person needs to have more of an ongoing role in the project.

Staying in Compliance with the SEC

The SEC regulates the sale of equities in all types of businesses. There are also security exchange oversight entities on the state level. The majority of their work involves large companies and publicly traded stocks. When you are bringing passive equity investors into your business, you are, in essence, selling them a share of your company, which *could* be a sale of a *security*.

So what defines a security? I spoke to my attorney about the SEC and its involvement in real estate transactions. We talked about the four-prong test that an investment must pass to be considered a security, requiring registration with the SEC. This test was established during a Supreme Court case in the 1940s, and it still upholds today. Here are the four prongs and my notes from the conversation I had with my attorney on them.

PRONG 1 | An investment of money

You may think that it would go without saying that money must change hands for an investment to be made. That's not necessarily the case in all circumstances, as other things could be exchanged in a business transaction, such as services, expertise, or just plain old sweat equity. Even if you didn't put money into your deal, your Cash Providers most likely did. Not all partners need to invest money, but as long as there is an investment of something of monetary value by at least one partner, this prong is satisfied.

PRONG 2 | In a common enterprise

An enterprise could be interpreted to mean a group of individuals or organizations working together toward a common goal. This could be under the formation of an LLC or other entity structure, or it could be two separate companies partnering on a venture, such as a tenant in common arrangement. The big differentiator is that the entities need to be on the same side of the transaction, meaning that they need to win and lose together. This prong is the one that removes private loans as qualifying for a security. In a loan, the parties are on opposing sides of the transaction. If the lender made more money, it came out of the borrower's pocket. If the borrower defaults, the lender can foreclose and take the property, which is surely not a win for the borrower. A private loan does not qualify as a common enterprise and because of this prong is disqualified as a security.

PRONG 3 | With the expectation of profits

Once again, this one may seem obvious, but it eliminates many other arrangements as being securities. Perhaps your uncle gifted you $10,000 for your new business. The money was a gift with no expectation of profit or a return of capital. The same goes for donations to a nonprofit. Any arrangement you enter into with a Cash Provider should have an expectation of profit, so in your business, this prong will be met.

PRONG 4 | Solely through the efforts of the promoter

It's through this prong that your equity deal will either qualify as a security or be disqualified. As in most legal definitions, the terms are vague and open to interpretation. In essence, this is aimed at passive investors who have no involvement or knowledge in the day-to-day actions of the company. I've done deals with a few partners, and we both had a role that brought about the company's goals. In some instances, my partners would personally guarantee the loan with me and I would catch them up on the progress of the business on a monthly basis. Their role was more peripheral, but I did make a point to discuss business decisions—like tenant applications, major maintenance, cash flow, and expense reduction—with them. The owners of the company don't need to have the same role; as long as all members are contributing in some way to the goals of the business, it's not a security. That said, if any of your investors have no role at all in the operation of the company or the advancement of its goals and are 100 percent passive, then your investment qualifies as a security according to this prong.

If the deal you are doing does not satisfy one of the prongs above, you do not have a security and no registration or exemption is required. If a sale of a security is involved, it's highly likely that you are exempt from registering it with the SEC. The SEC grants many exemptions to registration, but you need to make sure that your deal qualifies. I can't give you advice on whether or not you should file an exemption for every deal you do. You really need to talk to an attorney about these things. I can direct you to the SEC's website, which is very helpful and even has a link to register deals.[3]

While I won't get into whether or not you should file an exemption for specific deals, I will go over a few key points that will help keep you in compliance.

Preexisting Relationships

The SEC requires that all Cash Providers have a preexisting relationship with the Deal Provider. This relationship is not defined by time or any other factor aside from saying that it must be "substantive." I find it helpful to document all my interactions with my new investors and make sure that we discuss their goals first. If they are local, I will meet with them face-to-face if I can. Not only does this keep you in compliance with the SEC, but it also allows you to get to know their goals and allows them to get comfortable with you and your business plan before making a commitment to invest.

Solicitation

The SEC has very strict rules against soliciting for investors. Until recently, solicitations of any kind were prohibited. A solicitation is a public offering to invest with you, made to people you don't have a preexisting relationship with. I've even seen people post things on Facebook that could be interpreted as a solicitation. I find it better to not offer anything publicly. If you just have a conversation with the public on what you are up to, interested parties will come to you so you can establish a relationship. Post pictures of your fix-and-flips or your rental purchases, but don't follow them with "My investor made 15 percent on this deal. Send me a message if you want that return too." The bottom line here is to be careful with what you put out to the general public, and make sure it can't be misconstrued as a solicitation to invest with you.

As I said, solicitation is now allowed by companies that apply to do it prop-

---

3 Here are two helpful websites to get more information: www.sec.gov/smallbusiness/exemptofferings and www.sec.gov/answers/regd.htm.

erly and are approved by the SEC. The crowdfunding portals are an example of these companies. You may have seen their ads all over, offering returns on investment in everything from shopping mall investments to apartment complexes. It's important to note that, currently, companies that solicit for investors can take only accredited investors in their projects.

Accredited and Sophisticated Investors

The SEC has set up a benchmark for investors having to do with their income and their net worth. The thought process is that if people make above a certain amount of money or have a certain net worth, they have proved themselves to be financially astute and are allowed to invest in more complex offerings, like hedge funds, venture capital, and real estate equity deals. The benchmarks for being accredited are as follows. Investors must meet one of the following to qualify:

- An individual income of more than $200,000 per year, or a joint income of $300,000, in each of the past two years, with the expectation to reasonably maintain the same level of income going forward
- A net worth exceeding $1,000,000, either individually or jointly with a spouse. This figure excludes the equity in their primary residence.

Another option is for investors to state that they are *sophisticated investors*. In essence, they are stating that they have the knowledge and experience in financial matters that gives them the ability to evaluate your offering for its financial merit.

In most instances, your investors can just state which of these categories they fit in. For larger companies and ones that do solicitations, they need to verify that the investors are accredited before moving forward. While the SEC allows for investment from both accredited and sophisticated investors, there are rules on how much capital you can take from each of these types of investors.

Investor Qualification Forms

When investors come to us with an interest in investing, the first thing we do is ask them to fill out an investor qualification form. This form asks them to list out how they found us, what their goals for investment are, and what their timeline is. It helps us prove the relationship if it comes up, and it also helps us find a way to align with their goals. They also indicate if they are accredited or sophisticated and provide us an idea of how much investment capital they have available.

There is a lot more to the conversation around SEC compliance, but I really want to encourage you to get a solid attorney and perhaps a mentor who's a few steps ahead of you in real estate investing experience. Your attorney will look to protect you from the worst-case scenario (that's what attorneys do best)! Your mentor can give you a more realistic perspective and help you evaluate what to do based on experience.

Common Mistakes Made on Equity Deals

Before moving on, I want to caution you with a few common mistakes I've seen investors make when they put together equity arrangements with investors and active partners.

MISTAKE NO. 1 ❘ *Setting the Bar Too High*. I find that I'm most successful when I under-promise and over-deliver. In my earlier days, I would encounter a deal that looked like a slam dunk, so I would broadcast it as such to my investor base. The problem is that deals change as they unfold, and it's better to temper expectations. If you are writing up a projection for a rental deal, don't show the property at full performance right after closing. There will most likely be a ramp-up period, getting nonpaying tenants out and new ones in and completing renovations or other efforts to stabilize the property. It's better to account for this so that investors know what to expect. I can tell you it's better than their expecting a check in the first quarter of ownership.

MISTAKE NO. 2 ❘ *Going in Blind*. If you have equity investors lined up to work with you, it can be tempting to jump in by setting up an LLC with them and finding deals. This is called a blind fund, and it means you are going in with money but are blind on the deal you are going to take on. I would recommend against that unless you are very clear on the deal types and geography you are going to focus on. I have seen this model work when there are open lines of communication between the Deal Provider and the Cash Provider on the progress of finding the opportunities and whether the Cash Provider gets veto power if a deal comes up that doesn't seem to meet the criteria. This formation can also work if both investors are active, so they both are a part of finding and getting the deal performing.

MISTAKE NO. 3 ❘ *Not Being Clear on Roles*. I think this is the biggest mistake that you can make in an equity deal. Make sure that your Cash Providers are clear on what your role is and what their role is. I did an equity deal with one Cash Provider years ago where he put in the cash and I did the legwork, and we split the profit fifty-fifty. All was good until we went to refinance the property and the bank wanted a personal guarantee from him. This was a major problem for him, as he didn't want anything in his name. We ended up working around it and got the mortgage, but had I been clearer on this role he had as 50 percent owner, we could have avoided that conversation late in the game.

Another way that not being clear on roles shows up is with two active partners. I've had my own partnerships not work out because of lack of clarity, and I've seen investor friends of mine deal with the frustrations that arise from the simple disagreement of who is supposed to be doing what. Nailing this down up front is imperative with active partnerships and can cause resentment and potential business collapse if it's not dealt with.

Final Thoughts on Structuring Equity Deals

Here are a few final thoughts on structuring equity deals before we move on:

- Prospective Cash Providers will most likely want to do equity deals with you because of the perceived higher return on investment. Make sure you show them other options, as well, and consider doing a small private loan deal to get started with them.
- Have a good attorney who is affordable but knowledgeable on real estate transactions, equity, and deal structure. I can't stress this enough.
- Be clear on roles, goals, and compensation for all parties involved at all times.

CHAPTER 9
MANAGEMENT, EXITING, AND BEYOND

There is so much time and effort that goes into finding deals and Cash Providers to work with you on those deals. Once a deal is closed, funded, and structured, it can be tempting to get out and find the next opportunity. I have been guilty of the "What's next?" syndrome myself. As hard as you may have worked to get the deal funded and closed, you are at the very beginning of the process. True success in any investor deal comes from your working hard to make the vision you laid out for the deal come true and doing your best to exceed expectations. The real money is made in managing the deal ongoing and keeping it on track.

Investor Relations Plan

There is another exercise in *The 7 Habits of Highly Effective People* by Stephen Covey that really spoke to me. It's about recognizing things that are important or not important along with urgent or not urgent. Urgent tasks are the ones that are screaming at us, and important tasks are the ones that will put money in our pockets or otherwise advance us toward our long-term goals. Getting back to your broker about a hot deal with a bid deadline of tomorrow at noon is urgent and important. Sometimes when we are in reaction mode, we spend our time doing the things that are urgent but not important, like responding to emails or taking unscheduled phone calls.

Nothing is wrong with these things, but if we spend our whole day working on things that are urgent but not important, nothing important gets done. One of the great lessons of the book is that the key to success lies in doing the things that are important but *not* urgent. Those are the tasks that aren't screaming at us to get done because they aren't urgent, but doing them will contribute to our long-term growth, wealth, and purpose.

If you are like me, it's very easy to get sucked into the day-to-day reactivity. Once you have a few projects moving at once, it can become easy to just go after the loudest ringing bell, to just deal with squeaky wheels in your business. I have found that for me, the only way to keep on top of the important but not urgent tasks, and to make a real impact on my goals, is to use a good planning system. There are a ton of options out there, and I'm not going to recommend a specific personal organization system over another. What most of them boil down to is scheduling the important but not urgent tasks on your calendar ahead of time. This is an important habit to prevent going into reactive mode in your business and is necessary to implement what I'm going to recommend to you for keeping in touch with your Cash Providers.

Investor relations is one of those important but not urgent tasks that will make a world of difference in your business growth. I have found that a consistent system works for me when it comes to handling prospective investors and keeping in touch with current Cash Providers. That way, I have a consistent action to take when a new investor shows up, and I have a consistent action to keep in touch with current investors. That said, it's important to constantly look at how you are doing things, find ways to raise your game, and also accommodate your growing business. Some aspects of the system I will outline for you here are in place now in my business, while others are on the horizon for implementation. You may find that some suggestions I have are overkill for your current business size, but remember that it's better to have a more organized system that you can grow into than to quickly outgrow the one you are using.

The system involves actions you need to take on a daily, weekly, monthly, quarterly, and annual basis. Here we go:

Daily Actions

There are not many things you need to do from an investor management standpoint that have to be scheduled on a daily basis. However, there are things that can occur that you should respond to within twenty-four hours if you can, which will show your Cash Providers and prospects great customer service and increase your investor retention.

The first daily action may seem obvious to some; it's dealing with a call from a new prospective investor. You need to jump right on these leads. Most of the time, these come through an introduction from another active Cash Provider, but once you ramp up your social media efforts, these will come through those outlets also. For me, the lead usually comes via email or some other digital notification through our media outlets. It could be a comment on one of your blog posts or YouTube videos that seems to express interest. In whatever manner the potential interested party shows up, you should reply to the communication within twenty-four hours. When I get a new prospective Cash Provider, I do my best to put him or her into our lead funnel by getting an email address. I then send the person our new prospective investor email, which includes a brief summary of what we are up to as a company, a few videos taken from our active projects, what we offer to investors, and a link to fill out an investor qualification form.

The investor qualification form is a Google form that collects some data we need to help them, such as their investment goals, timeline, investment capacity, types of deals they have done in the past, etc. I also make it clear that we offer passive investments like private loans, turnkeys, and positions in equity deals to those who qualify. You may get inquiries from people who don't fit your mold, so make it clear what you offer up front to screen out the prospects who are looking for something you don't offer.

The second action that you should complete within twenty-four hours is responding to investor communications or other investor urgent matters. Again, it's about customer service. It could be a simple question like "When do we get our data for our tax returns from you?" Or "What's the address of that deal we talked about, again?" It doesn't matter what their question is. If you can, have a one-business-day response time for all investor communications, no matter what they are. At times, investors will need your help urgently. I once had one of my investors buy a house, and for some reason, his bank waited until the last minute to get a statement of his investment activities with me. He was a day away from closing and had to have this, or he wouldn't close on his home purchase. Of course, I dropped what I was doing and helped him get his purchase closed.

Weekly Actions

The daily interactions we talked about are typically quick responses or getting back to leads. There is not much prep work needed in them, and the interactions are typically short. Much of your investor relationship-building activity will occur on a weekly basis. These longer interactions should be prepared for in advance.

For new prospects, I send an intro email and my qualification form as soon as they make contact. Once I get their investor qualification form back, I review it and send them a link to set up a phone or video call. I use a service called Calendly to set up my calls. There are other services like it out there as well. They offer specific time blocks you have set aside for investor calls to your prospects, allowing them to pick which one works for them. It then drops the meeting into my calendar with all the contact info for the call and sends them an invite; it even reminds them before the meeting. I try to have this call with a new prospect within one week of their completing the qualification form to keep things moving. On the call, I learn about their goals and discuss more about how my company can help them get where they want to go. We talk about their experience in passive investments and review a few of our projects. We also talk about what cash sources they have. Many are not aware that they can use their IRA for investment activity, so I'm sure to mention how powerful an SDIRA can be as a real estate investment tool.

While we are on the call, I am constantly taking notes in our investor database so that I can reference it in the future. Like I mentioned earlier, I use software called Podio because it's cost-effective and allows me to tailor it to my needs. I put as much into their profile on Podio as I can from our conversation. If they really want to get into turnkeys and want to start with a duplex, I now have that data so I can support them when the right deal comes up. If they won't be ready to invest for six months or so, I can use Podio to remind me to reach out to them later.

If they are ready to get moving and I am comfortable that we have established a relationship, I will offer up some projects we have in the works. When the investor is local to me, I will try to set up a face-to-face meeting and a tour of one of our jobsites. I always try to get a follow-up from the initial call, even if it's just adding them to our newsletter and following up again in six months.

Another activity that you should set aside time for weekly is calls for funding new deals. This is especially true of the smaller fix-and-flip deals or BRRRR deals in need of a Cash Provider to step in as a lender. If you are just getting started, you may not need to do this every week. Once you start developing a pipeline of deals and Cash Providers, you will need to set aside time to search your database for the right fit for your pending projects. If I can wait a bit, I also try to share these deals that need a Cash Provider to our investor database via our monthly newsletter, but sometimes we need to close in a week or two and can't wait until the next release date.

As you get into larger projects and equity deals, you will want to set aside a time to present to multiple investors on an opportunity at once. The best way I've found to do this is via a weekly scheduled webinar. In the webinar, you can present the marketing material for your deal, make sure all the key points get covered, and even take live questions from the attendees. You can also record the webinar and send the recording to others who are interested. When you are raising for a specific deal, odds are you will be on a tight timeline, so you should stack a few of these webinars in your weekly schedule and also set aside time to make follow-up calls to those who attended.

Another weekly activity is updating your social media and digital marketing feeds. You can't be sporadic with your posts. You have to keep new content coming out weekly if you want to build a following. You won't see results right away either. We had less than 100 subscribers when we first started our YouTube channel. Once we committed to using this platform consistently, we began to post two videos a week and haven't changed that rhythm once. Over time we continued to add content, and eventually people started to notice. You can do the same with a podcast, a blog, a Facebook group, or other means to get your voice out there. Just make sure that your posts are regular, predictable, and repeatable.

Monthly Actions

Aside from your follow-ups with prospective investors, your monthly actions will likely be broken down into two regular tasks. The first is sending out project status updates to everyone who's a Cash Provider involved in your short-term deals. This includes your lenders on your fix-and-flips or BRRRR deals or other Cash Providers who you are currently working with on projects that have a timeline of less than twelve months. If you have a long-term rental project that is not yet stabilized, meaning it's still under renovation and not fully leased, send those Cash Providers a monthly update also. The update should include the status of the project, pictures and a video update if you can, and a current timeline. If you are slightly off budget or off timeline, let them know. If you are way off, give them a call. As I said in an earlier chapter, you need to let them know, as no one likes a surprise when it comes to their money.

Another monthly action I take to keep in touch with my current and potential investors is sending out a well-thought-out newsletter. I love newsletters for a bunch of reasons. They allow me to keep in touch with my investor base in one action. I can send out updates on projects they are involved in and put new deals in front of them. On another angle, I get regular contact with new investors who haven't gotten on board yet. The database software I use connects to my newsletter software, so whenever I put in new contacts, they go right into my distribution list. The newsletter service I use allows me to see who clicks on which link or who deleted it without opening the email. I once sent out a newsletter about a new deal we were working on. One of my active Cash Providers clicked on the link for that project five times. You'd better believe he got a phone call that day! The last reason I love newsletters is that they can be forwarded to others. You never know who knows other people who may want to hear more about you. The newsletter model makes it easy for your database to spread the word about you.

In each of my newsletters, I highlight:

- **Long-Term Rental Deals** – I will put an update in for one or two of these projects. We have more than that active, but once these deals are stabilized, we don't see much change month to month. For these properties, we will include some photos, a video if I have one, and a brief write-up including some performance numbers.
- **Short-Term Deals** – If I have a flip or a BRRRR active, I will show an update on it, as people love to see properties like this in transition.
- **Educational Content** – I want to give value to anyone who reads the newsletter, even those who aren't invested with us, so I include a few video educational tips.
- **Info on a New Deal** – If I have something in the works that may be of interest to a Cash Provider, I will include this information as well. It's important to not make this section sound like a solicitation, both for SEC purposes and also because you don't want to be pushy about it. I will just put in the details on a deal we are doing and a link they can click on to get more info. If they click the link, it takes them to a page with more information and allows them to register for an upcoming webinar.

Quarterly Actions

Getting back to new contacts quickly, searching for money for new deals, and keeping in touch with your database are activities that need to occur frequently. On the other side, there are actions that don't need to occur as often but are just as important. What will set you apart is the ability to do the less frequent but more thought-out actions with your investors.

Let's talk about your long-term hold deals. At first, they may need to be renovated and leased out, which would warrant monthly communications with your database. Once they are stabilized, leased, and cash-flowing, there is not as much to talk about. At that point, you can drop back to sending a quarterly update consisting of a financial report and summary. You should be using financial accounting software that is able to create a profit-and-loss statement and a balance sheet at minimum. I will typically run a report in Excel and then add more detail to it or make it more understandable to my investor database. I send this to them by email along with a brief summary on how the past three months of ownership went and any plans for the immediate future.

I find that once a quarter, we typically encounter a full cycle of expenses on a rental deal. Real estate taxes are typically billed that often, as are water, sewer, and other municipal fees. I set my insurance up to bill quarterly as well. From a maintenance perspective, one quarter will take you through one season. Each season tends to have its own maintenance expenses, such as shoveling snow, cutting grass, weeding, pest management, roof repairs, etc. For all these reasons, I feel that we have a good financial picture after a quarter of ownership and can look at our cash flow and issue an owner profit draw. We typically don't distribute every dime we make. I will set aside a percentage of cash flow or a certain amount of dollars per unit for capital expenses. This is a fancy way of saving up money to replace the expensive items like roofs, heaters, windows, sidewalks, and others things that would kill your cash flow if you performed them without saving up. Once I take out some money for that, I will take the rest and send it to the Cash Provider as a dividend, which is broken up by their percentage of ownership. If they own 23.5 percent of the deal, they get that percentage of the cash flow. This percentage of profit is one of the many things defined in the operating agreement you used when you structured the deal with them.

Annual Actions

Once you get into larger projects like midsize apartment building deals with a large group of investors, you will want to have an annual conference call. You can also have a face-to-face with all your investors if they are local. On that call or in that meeting, you should review the previous year's activity and compare it with your goals and budget you had for that period. You should also talk about your plans for the short and long terms for the property and present the budget projection for the following year. Investors will expect this level of communication on larger deals, and it will benefit you if you practice these conversations on your smaller projects as you grow into larger ones.

The next annual action you need to take is preparing your investors' documents for their taxes. As you already know, I am not a CPA, and you should have a CPA in your corner who works regularly with real estate and partnership deals. For your equity investors, I'm assuming they own a percentage of an LLC with you. All owners of an LLC get a K-1 document, showing the taxable profit they made through owning this company with you. Those who invested in a joint venture with you will be owed tax documents, as well, most likely a 1099. Those to whom you paid interest will get a special 1099 for that interest. If you are using some other ownership structure we haven't discussed in this book, you may have other documents to send them for tax time.

Other Thoughts on Investor Relations

Not everyone communicates the same way. Some like face-to-face conversations, others like phone calls, and others want it all in writing. It helps to figure out what kind of communicator each of your investors is. Some of my investors will respond right away if I send them a text message or call them on their cell. Others want everything in detailed emails so they can digest it and get back to me with their thoughts. Some of my investors watch the videos I post to keep up with their projects. Others have never watched one of my videos or opened one newsletter, but they will call me back in twenty-four hours or less if I call them. When you are first getting to know your new investors, ask them how they prefer to get their communication from you. Also notice how quickly people get back to you when you send them a certain type of communication. I find that people respond fastest when you send them their favorite means of communication. Take note of what they respond to, and keep communicating with them in the means that work best for them.

Another point I want to make is that your investors will start to notice if the only time you call them is when you need money for a deal. Try to find a reason to reach out. Perhaps you start a program to call them on their birthday. You could put a note in your calendar to call one of your Cash Providers every Tuesday at three in the afternoon. Just go down the list and call one a week, just to check in. You never know what will come up in conversation. Maybe a lead for a new investor or maybe a deal they heard about that needs a buyer. Either way, stay in front of them, and keep you and your company fresh in their mind.

I should point out that all these actions are only for investor management.

There should be a whole other list of actions you take to keep your deal pipeline full, manage your current projects, and keep your overall business healthy. I find that breaking down the facets of my business into daily weekly, monthly, quarterly, and annual lists like these helps me compartmentalize the business and makes sure those important but not urgent activities get done.

Exit Strategies

Unwinding your deal can seem so far off in the future when you first set it up. Even on a six-month fix-and-flip project, thinking about how you are going to get the Cash Provider his or her money back at the end may not be your first thought. I can tell you that even on the longer deals, the end can creep up on you quickly, so you should always begin with the end in mind.

Exiting Private Loans

As I reviewed in Chapter 7, unwinding a private loan deal can be as simple as getting your Cash Providers their interest and principal back at closing. I hope it's that simple for you. If you buy right, do a great job estimating your construction cost, and keep the project on time and on budget, and if the market behaves itself while you are under renovation, you will end up just fine and hit your profit target. That's a lot of ifs, though. Perhaps you have to fire your general contractor because he stops showing up on your job. I've fired plenty of general contractors in my years of business, and it's always cost me time and money. I had a few flips going when the market crashed in 2008. I was able to convert them into rentals. They didn't cash-flow very much, if at all, but at least I didn't lose them to foreclosure. I still own a few, just paying down the mortgage with the tenants' rent until the principal balance drops enough to a point that it makes sense to sell them. If your fix-and-flip or BRRRR deal goes to sell or refinance and you can't get the lender out 100 percent, here are some options, all of which should be addressed in your loan documents before getting started.

- Have some of your own cash on the sidelines ready to pay off your lender. Once you are established, this shouldn't be a problem. Just make sure you didn't have that cash committed to another project. Don't rob Peter to pay Paul.
- Convert the overage to unsecured debt. If your loan is $100,000 in principal plus $5,000 in interest, and you net $90,000 after commissions from the sale, see whether your lender will convert the remaining $15,000 to an un-

secured loan with you as the personal guarantor. You will need to show how you can make monthly payments on the loan until it's paid and will also need to offer some sort of interest rate on the lender's money while you pay him or her off. On a BRRRR deal, you may be able to offer a second mortgage on the property and pay the lender back with monthly payments over time.

- Roll your lenders into another deal. If they believe in you and want to give you another shot, this may be the best option. Remember, your lenders can become strategic partners of yours and stick with you for years and years. Jumping in to help you out of a jam like this works for them, too, if they are committed to your long-term success as someone helping them build their wealth. As in the example above, you owe them $15,000, and they have $90,000 of their loan capital back. Perhaps you can put them into your next flip deal, with them getting the first $15,000 of the profit plus interest on that money.
- If it's a BRRRR deal, convert them to equity. This plan can get tricky if the deal is held in an LLC that owns other properties and/or has other owners. The way it works is the overage you owe them gets converted to a percentage of ownership of the rental property, giving them rights to some of the cash flow and profit on sale. You may even be able to work out a way to pay them off over time with cash flow to get the equity back.

Exiting Joint Ventures

Winding up a joint venture deal is very similar to doing so in a loan project, except your joint venture partner gets a chunk of the profit on the fix-and-flip. On these deals, make sure that all the expenses that get deducted from the sales revenue get taken out when you calculate the profit that gets split up. Things like their interest payment or a construction management fee for you may get neglected at first glance. Also, don't forget that the equity that went into the deal up front is not profit; it's their seed capital.

Let's say your joint venture partner puts $100,000 into a flip deal. You commit to giving 8 percent on his or her money plus 15 percent of the profit. You borrow $300,000 from a bank for an acquisition and construction loan, taking you up to $400,000 in obligations. You sell the property after six months of ownership and net $250,000 in cash after the bank loan is paid off. You take a $10,000 construction management fee and owe the lender $100,000 times 8 percent per year, times 6 months, equaling $4,000 in interest. Net cash back after sale is $236,000. Give your partner back his or her $100,000 first and then split the $136,000, not the total cash back from the sale. Your joint venture partner's total profit is $4,000 in interest plus 15 percent times $136,000, or $20,400, which equals $24,400 in profit—a 24.4 percent return on the partner's money on a six-month deal. Not bad, and you made a nice profit plus a management fee for yourself too.

Not every joint venture deal is a slam dunk like the one above. If the deal is not as profitable, it only drops the partner's percentage of profit. Remember, you should not be committing to a certain return on the money on these deals aside from the base interest rate. If partners want the rights to the upside potential on the deal, they need to know that they are also subjecting themselves to a lower return if the deal doesn't profit as well. As long as you can meet their base interest rate on the payoff, you have met your obligation to them. If the profit on sale isn't able to meet even the interest payment or, even worse, get them all their money back, you may need to go with one of the options I listed above for loans. Make sure your joint venture agreement is solid and addresses these potential outcomes.

Exiting Equity Deals

Exiting an equity deal can be more complex compared with other arrangements with your Cash Providers. These are typically long-term hold deals, and many Cash Providers get into them for the tax advantages. When you sell the property, all those tax advantages can get turned into a large tax obligation. If you are taking a large depreciation write-off during ownership and you sell for a profit, you need to pay back all those depreciation deductions you took during ownership, which is called depreciation recapture.

Aside from getting very complex with buyout structures, the most common way out of an equity deal is a sale. You can also try to negotiate for a buyout for your investors through a refinance; just make sure the terms of the buyout include how much compensation they will get for their ownership, which should be extremely clear in your operating agreement. If your deal is profitable and the property goes up significantly in value, you want to make sure your terms are clear, as your Cash Providers may not want to let their ownership in the property go very easily.

If you can get all your Cash Providers to agree, you can do a 1031 exchange on the sale. In essence, this is trading up into a larger deal, taking all the sales proceeds and rolling them into the purchase of a new property. There are tight time constraints on 1031 exchanges, limiting how long you have between the sale of the subject property and the purchase of the replacement. You have to move quickly, or you will be subject to paying tax on the sale, and there are no extensions. Most investors I know who have done a 1031 start looking for the replacement deal as soon as the subject property goes under agreement. As I said, all your Cash Providers need to agree to do a 1031. If any Cash Provider objects to being rolled into a new project that was outside the original scope, you can't move forward with a 1031.

In circumstances like this, you can offer to have investors who want to continue with you buy out the ones who want out. As long as both sides are reasonable with their offers for the ownership shares in question, it can be a win-win arrangement.

It Can Get Complicated (in a Good Way)

A few years ago, I came across a deal for an eighteen-unit apartment building in Philadelphia. The man who owned it had built it himself forty years earlier and held it ever since. He was getting older and wanted to get out of the land-lord business. The building had a fire a few years earlier, which caused most of the tenants to move out. Although the owner used the insurance settlement wisely and renovated the building, he didn't want to deal with leasing the building back out and was at 50 percent occupancy when we looked at it. It was in a quiet suburban neighborhood just on the edge of town. Most of the residents wanted to stay but were paying well below market rents. A typical one-bedroom went for $750 in that area; he was getting $500. He owned it free and clear, so most of the profit went into his pocket, and he was happy to get the revenue for not much headache. We agreed on a price of $1,050,000. I was able to get a mortgage for $680,000, leaving me $500,000 to raise from investors, considering closing costs and up-front renovations. I was able to pull together eight investors with an average investment of $75,000. I setup an LLC with investors getting 65 percent and my company holding 35 percent of the deal. We closed the deal in around ninety days from the first time we walked it.

I managed the property with our own team, as it was only thirty min-utes from my office. With some hard work, we were able to get it fully leased in about six months. Investors knew there would be a ramp-up period and were OK not getting proceeds checks while we were in development. Over the years, we continued to raise rents and do what we could to keep expenses down. The property cash-flowed nicely, and investors were happy. During that time, I had been working more on turnkey projects and met a group of investors who looked at a four-family I had for sale. They didn't like that one because they wanted to do a larger deal. They asked me about other properties in our portfolio, and I mentioned the one in Philadelphia. I had no desire to sell it, as we had owned it for only a few years and it was performing well.

Every month or so, that investment group would send me an email, asking whether I would consider selling. I kept telling them no but thanked them for their interest. I had been thinking about refinancing the building to make some capital improvements, like upgrading the hallways, putting in new windows, and replacing the boiler or separating heating systems to save on expenses. When I ran the numbers on our performance, I saw the building would value at $1,500,000 based on its income. Around that time, the investment group sent me an email that pretty much said, "We know you don't want to sell. But is there a price that would make you change your mind?" I told them $1,500,000, and they immediately sent me an agreement of sale. I ran the numbers and called one of my key investors. If we sold at that number, we would net $700,000, which yielded an internal rate of return for our investors of more than 20 percent on their money per year. I couldn't pass it up and signed the agreement to move forward.

The problem we faced was that this was supposed to be a five- to seven-year hold, and we were on year three. Investors were happy with the return we were getting for them, but none of them wanted their money back. I had to find them something else. We had just put the deal under agreement for sale, and I immediately started looking for the second half of the 1031 exchange.

We had been growing our deal size and were beyond looking at eighteen units. We were now chasing a 198-unit deal in North Carolina. The problem was that this was a much larger deal, requiring $3,200,000 in equity from investors. I wanted to know whether it would be possible to invest the sales profit as a 1031 exchange into the larger deal, contributing the $700,000 in sales proceeds as an investment in the property. I was very intrigued by this, as it would allow the sale of the building in Philadelphia to contribute 20 percent of the equity to the deal in one swoop. It also satisfied our investors and kept their capital moving.

I did some homework and found out that it was possible through something called a tenant in common arrangement, or TIC. This is a certain way that the property needs to be held in title, which allowed us to hold title jointly between the new company and the one performing the 1031 exchange. There could be a whole other book on the TIC process and how it plays into 1031 exchange law, so just know that it's possible. Although it got complex, it was a win. I was able to complete the sale of the property in Philadelphia successfully and didn't need to raise as much for the new purchase.

When Someone Needs Out Early

You should have been extremely clear with your Cash Providers that equity deals are long-term holds that don't have exact, defined exit dates. Additionally, getting their cash back for their shares can be difficult, if not impossible. The money should be viewed as tied up long term to produce growth and dividends for them, not something liquid that they can cash in easily. All of this should have been covered with them in conversation and further agreed to by them in the legal documents they signed to get on board with you in the project.

Although you did this, it's likely that at some point, you will have Cash Providers come to you and want to talk about how they can get their money back. Perhaps they had an unforeseen personal expense or a change in their financial situation. Perhaps they want to start their own business or are cashing in all their investments. For whatever reason, they want to create cash from their shares. As I covered in Chapter 8, your operating agreement needs to have a "member exit" clause, allowing them to sell their shares.

The way this normally goes is, the Cash Provider notifies you in writing that he or she wants to sell the shares. You then contact the rest of the investors and notify them that another member wants to sell. Keep everything anonymous, of course. Those interested will make an offer for the shares, which the seller can accept, decline, or counter. If no agreement can be reached, you have the right to make an offer on the shares also. If the seller again declines your offer, he or she can go out and find a third party to buy the shares of the company. Perhaps a contact of the seller's is interested, or the Cash Provider finds a buyer through a broker who sells shares in real estate investments. If the investor gets an acceptable offer, he or she brings this price back to you and each of the other investors, and you get the right to match that offer and buy the shares. If no one does so, the third party gets the shares and the seller gets the sales proceeds. This process may sound complicated, but it's the fairest way to go about it, and it also allows the current owners to do their best to keep the ownership in-house.

Beyond the Deal

To be successful long term in this business, you need to think beyond the deals. You need to think beyond the Cash Providers also. At the core of everything, it's really about who you want to become through the process of building a real estate empire and whom you want to serve in the process.

And maybe you don't want an empire. There is nothing wrong with keeping your portfolio small and manageable, looking to have it paid off by the time you retire so you can live off the income.

Short- and Long-Term Goals

Whatever you are looking to build, make sure you set some inspiring yet attainable goals for yourself and build a business plan to achieve those goals. I suggest that you have one-, three-, and five-year goals for yourself—and for the benefit of your Cash Providers to see where you're headed. It's hard to stay focused without short- and long-term goals. Take it from me. I know. When I first got started in this business, I didn't have clear goals on where I wanted to go, and I didn't go anywhere. It wasn't until I got clear on what I wanted and how I was going to get there that things started happening for me.

Start with the five-year goal. Almost anything can happen in five years. I know investors who got started five years ago and now own thousands of units. I know people who got in five years ago and are now retired. Your five-year goal can be whatever you want it to be, so think big. Don't make it all about money either. Think about the *life* you want to be leading five years from now. What are you doing day to day? Where do you live? Provide as much detail on this vision as you can, and then start to think about what real estate business you need to have in place to allow you to lead that life. List the accomplishments in your business that got you there too. How many flips? How many rentals? What kind of Cash Providers are working with you?

Once you have your five-year goal vision down, think about where you are now and what needs to happen between now and year five. Your three-year goal should be a midpoint between here and there, so put together a three-year goal set with the same level of detail that bridges the gap from where you are standing today and where you want to be. Although the five-year vision may seem like a million miles away, the three-year should seem a bit closer and act as a transition point for you. Again, how many deals have you done, what does your business look like at this milestone, and whom are you partnered with?

You need to do the same for your one-year vision. This is where you may not see huge transformation in your life compared with your current situation, but you will be laying the foundation for the five-year vision for yourself. The plan to get to your one-year goal should be very detailed and measurable so you can start implementing it immediately. If you want to really drill down, you can take your one-year goal and break it down into measurable achievements by month—and even by week and by day. If you are looking to build a sustainable business over the years, then start building the groundwork today that will support what you want to have in place in the future.

I sit down with my wife every year and vision out the next five years of our lives using this process. We check our progress on our long-term goals and re-vision where we want to go long term to make sure it still inspires us. We also meet once a quarter to check in on how we are doing, create our action plan, and course-correct as needed. We tweak our goals as needed for many reasons. When we had our first child, you'd better believe our goals changed. When the market shifted in 2008, we changed our goals then also. A wise man once told me that you cannot change the market; you can only participate in it. If the real estate market changes, you will need to adjust your goals to accommodate it and find a way to get where you want to go given the current market conditions.

Above all else, have the courage to say no when something comes up that is not in line with your long-term goals. I said yes to too many of these things when I first got started, and it stunted my growth. There are plenty of shiny nickels to chase out there. It may be exciting to talk about the next big thing, but I promise you there will *always* be a next big thing, a deal of the decade. Don't let it suck you away from your long-term vision.

Doing Whatever It Takes

There are many keys to success, but I think one of the core secrets to being successful in real estate investment and raising private money, and perhaps anywhere, is the desire to keep pushing and not quit. This business has offered me incentive to quit many times over the years, and I've just kept pushing. Getting through the hard times with a smile and finding solutions to all problems is what I mean by not quitting. Getting up and trying again when you fail. Asking for help. All of these are actions you need to take, but it's all under the commitment that you won't quit, no matter what.

I'm not sure about other businesses, but there are quite a few shady characters in the real estate business. I've met many of them—from the contractor who was just looking to get my initial deposit so he could disappear to the wholesaler who misrepresented a deal just to get a quick closing. If you stay in this business long enough, you will run into one of these folks. I don't wish this on you, but you may get taken by one of them. If it happens while you are working with Cash Providers' capital, you will need to be prepared to do the right thing on their behalf.

Remember the sale of that apartment building in Philadelphia? We were lined up for closing, and I needed to find a 1031 exchange intermediary to hold our sales proceeds to be rolled into the next deal. I did some research and found a company that was highly recommended on several online sites and had a very professional-sounding staff when I called them. Their fees were reasonable, as well, so I signed up. We closed the sale, and I wired them $700,000 in proceeds. I got regular communications from their office, letting me know the next steps of the process, and spoke to them several times to confirm we were on track. Finally, it came time to get things lined up for the purchase of the new building in North Carolina. When I called their office, I got only voice mails and no callbacks. I called a few more times and even asked my attorney to send them a stern email because we were getting closer to the day of closing. No response. I did more digging and finally reached another investor who had 1031 money in escrow with the same company. He had done more investigation and filled me in. Unfortunately, I had been duped by a con artist. This company had been running a Ponzi scheme for years, taking the 1031 proceeds from people's sales and using that money to build its own real estate investment business. It just so happened that the house of cards had fallen apart just before I needed the funds for my closing.

My heart sank. I didn't know what to do at first—get in the car and drive to their offices a few states away? Call the FBI? Curl up in the fetal position and cry my eyes out? All of these crossed my mind. It was a rough couple of days in figuring things out, but I knew one thing—my investors would be made whole, no matter what. I was a custodian of their money, and it was my duty to defend them.

The money was slated to go into our new apartment building purchase. The investors in that project would get 70 percent ownership; I would get 30 percent. I needed to raise $3,200,000 to close the deal, and the 1031 exchange money was part of that. I had raised the other $2,500,000 already and had some other investors lined up to get into the deal also. I had two problems to solve. The first was how to get the funds to close with a week left until closing. I had exhausted most of our investor network to get to this point and didn't have too many more prospects. I dug deep into my contact base, pounded the phones for two days, and was able to raise some more investors and also found a short-term bridge loan (similar to hard money) to get to closing. It was hard work, and there were some stressful moments, but I got it done.

The second problem was the harder one. How did I cover my investors from the 1031 exchange? This was an obvious answer to me but not an easy one. There was 30 percent of ownership for me and my team in the deal. Had the 1031 cash made its way into the deal, they would have purchased around 18 percent of the project. I had to give them the majority of my ownership to get them covered. It was the right thing to do but hard nonetheless. I had been working this deal for the past six months and would be on it for another five to ten years. Giving away two-thirds of my ownership didn't seem fair for the work I had to put in, but I had to do it. It was the only option to guarantee that their equity got protected. They will get the cash flow I would have gotten from the deal, and when we go to sell in the future, they will be the beneficiaries of it.

Regarding the pursuit of the company that took our money, I was able to line up a legal team and joined many other investors who had been taken by this company in a class action suit. It's still ongoing as of spring 2018, but there is strong promise, as we have been able to locate many of the real estate investments purchased by the company, many of which were bought free and clear. It will take some time and money, but I think we will get at least some of the lost capital back.

I sincerely hope that something like this never happens to you. This story is a painful one for me to relive, but I needed to share it with you here because I need to ask you this question: *Are you prepared to do whatever it takes for your Cash Providers?* It may not go down as it did in this story, but I can assure you that at some point in your business, you will have to choose your investors over yourself. Will you sacrifice your own profit, income, and hard work for them if you have to? Will you put them above yourself if that's what it takes to protect them? If you are not sure that you can do it, you should reconsider raising investors for your real estate business.

Final Thoughts

As this book comes to a close, there are a few thoughts I want to share with you. If you didn't get anything else from this book, I hope these points sink in, as they are key beliefs you need to have in this business to be successful.

Don't Ever Forget They Need You

Some people get hung up or embarrassed when they think about asking other people for money. This feeling can be intense when there is a close friend or family member sitting across the table. Remember: You are *not* asking them for money. You are offering them an opportunity. Through you, and your business, they can become wealthy. You can show them returns that don't exist elsewhere, and especially not on the roller coaster called the stock market. They need you. To reach their financial goals, they need someone they like and trust who has a solid plan and the resources and drive to bring that plan to fruition. It's your job to educate them first, then offer opportunities for win-win arrangements that take you both toward your goals.

Treat Their Money like Gold

Don't ever take your Cash Providers' money for granted or take unnecessary risks with it. If you wouldn't do it with your own money, don't do it with theirs. They have entrusted you with their livelihood. In some cases, it's their retirement accounts or their children's college funds or the life work of their parents who left it to them as a legacy. See yourself as they most likely see you: a custodian of their money and a trusted adviser who can help them achieve their financial goals. You can help them create real transformation for their family. You can help them become millionaires. Take this role with the high level of responsibility that it deserves.

Play the Long Game

This business gets painted with the wrong brush by some of the gurus out there. They paint a picture of starting up and, in no time, getting six-figure checks, living in mansions, and driving fancy cars. While some people get lucky out of the gate, this is not a "make millions in a month or two and then move to Tahiti" kind of business. You can have the big house and a fancy car as a goal and even have living in Tahiti on your list. However, what the gurus don't tell you is that there is a mountain of hard work, personal transformation, growth, hard knocks, lessons, laughs, and tears in between here and where you want to go.

You will get there, as long as you learn to play the long game. This means committing to staying in this business for the long haul, until you hit those long-term goals of yours. Make decisions based on your long-term goals, build a business that is designed to last a long time, and don't take the quick buck if it means burning a bridge to get to it. Those who don't get this concept are constantly crawling over people to get one more inch of profit, and they rarely have long-term business relationships with anyone. The problem with that is word gets around quickly, and it can take a lifetime to live down a bad reputation. The same goes for people who play the long game. Word gets out that you are someone who looks out for others and builds and forges win-wins.

Find a Recipe That Works and Stick with It

One of the mistakes I made early on in my business was getting my hands into too many different types of deals when I was a novice at all of them. There was a time when I was buying an office building, renovating a few small apartments, building a house, and using my license to represent a few rental property sellers. It was a mess, and a few of those projects didn't go too well because I lacked focus. Had I stuck to one thing and gotten great at it, then added another layer to my business, I would have grown much faster. I suggest that you look at your goals and find one or two real estate strategies that will get you to your one-year milestone. Then go as deep as you can, learning as much as possible while you keep your blinders on and implementing what you learn. Find a mentor in that space. Start a local mastermind group. Get super-focused on that area and master it, and then (and only then) add on another area of the business if it serves your long-term goals.

Above all else, don't forget to have some fun while you are at it. This can be a very rewarding business, but it can be fun too. Enjoy it, and realize how many lives that you have the chance to affect as an investor. The mantra for my company, the DeRosa Group, is "Transforming Lives Through Real Estate." When you think about it, that's what all of us are doing. We are making a difference in the lives of other people. That could be the life of a tenant in one of your rentals, an employee of your company, or someone who buys one of your flips and makes it the home to raise a family in. Of course, you are also helping others create wealth through working with you as your Cash Providers. Take honor in the role that real estate investing provides: that of making a real difference in people's lives through your business.

Acknowledgments

I would like to take a moment to thank a few people.

To Brandon Turner and Josh Dorkin for taking a shot on Liz and me a few years ago to write articles for BiggerPockets. Thank you for giving us a chance. It's been a phenomenal experience working with you and the team at BiggerPockets.

To Scott Trench, Katie Askew, Allison Leung, Zachary Gwin, Dave Meyers, Jarrod Jemison, and the team at BiggerPockets. Thanks for your endless support in making this book move from an idea to reality. Thank you to the editors: Taylor Hugo, Paul Silverman, and Katelin Hill. And thanks to Wendy Dunning for making the interior of this book look beautiful.

To my team at the DeRosa Group for holding down the fort while I poured my heart and soul into this book. Thanks for keeping things running so I could take the time to create this.

To my very first investors, my mother and father, and my in-laws. You have "invested" in Liz and me since birth. Thank you for making us who we are and for believing in us when we were just getting started.

To my very first nonfamily member investors, Michael and Steve. Thank you for believing in me so many years ago.

And finally, to all the real estate investors out there reading this who are looking to build a bigger business for yourself, your families, and those who work with you. I acknowledge you for stretching yourself and hope this book gives you what you need to take things to the next level!

More from
BiggerPockets Publishing

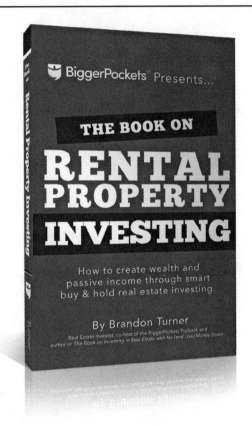

The Book on Rental Property Investing
With nearly 400 pages of in-depth advice and strategies for building wealth through rental properties, *The Book on Rental Property Investing* by BiggerPockets podcast cohost Brandon Turner will teach you how to build an achievable plan, find incredible deals, pay for your rentals, and much more! If you ever thought of using rental properties to build wealth or obtain financial freedom, this book is for you.

If you enjoyed this book, we hope you'll take a moment to check out some of the other great material BiggerPockets offers. BiggerPockets is the real estate investing social network, marketplace, and information hub, designed to help make you a smarter real estate investor through podcasts, books, blog posts, videos, forums, and more. Sign up today—it's free! **Visit www. BiggerPockets.com.**

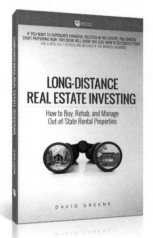

Long-Distance Real Estate Investing

Don't let your location dictate your financial freedom: Live where you want, and invest anywhere it makes sense! The rules, technology, and markets have changed: No longer are you forced to invest only in your backyard. In *Long-Distance Real Estate Investing*, learn an in-depth strategy to build profitable rental portfolios through buying, managing, and flipping out-of-state properties from real estate investor and agent David Greene.

The Book on Investing in Real Estate with No (and Low) Money Down

Lack of money holding you back from real estate success? It doesn't have to! In this groundbreaking book from Brandon Turner, author of *The Book on Rental Property Investing*, you'll discover numerous strategies investors can use to buy real estate using other people's money. You'll learn the top strategies that savvy investors are using to buy, rent, flip, or wholesale properties at scale!

More from
BiggerPockets Publishing

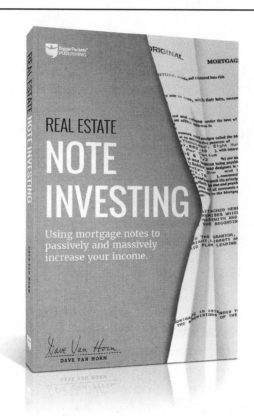

Real Estate Note Investing

Are you a wholesaler, a rehabber, a landlord, or even a turnkey investor? *Real Estate Note Investing* will help you turn your focus to the "other side" of real estate investing, allowing you to make money without tenants, toilets, and termites! Investing in notes is the easiest strategy to make passive income. Learn the ins and outs of notes as investor Dave Van Horn shows you how to get started—and find huge success—in the powerful world of real estate notes!

The Book on Tax Strategies for the Savvy Real Estate Investor

Taxes! Boring and irritating, right? Perhaps. But if you want to succeed in real estate, your tax strategy will play a huge role in how fast you grow. A great tax strategy can save you thousands of dollars a year. A bad strategy could land you in legal trouble. That's why BiggerPockets is excited to offer *The Book on Tax Strategies for the Savvy Real Estate Investor*! You'll find ways to deduct more, invest smarter, and pay far less to the IRS!

Set for Life: Dominate Life, Money, and the American Dream

Looking for a plan to achieve financial freedom in just five to ten years? *Set for Life* is a detailed fiscal plan targeted at the median-income earner starting with few or no assets. It will walk you through three stages of finance, guiding you to your first $25,000 in tangible net worth, then to your first $100,000, and then to financial freedom. *Set for Life* will teach you how to build a lifestyle, career, and investment portfolio capable of supporting financial freedom to let you live the life of your dreams.

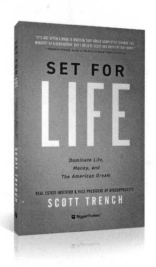

Learn More from
BIGGERPOCKETS

and Become Successful in
Your Real Estate Business Today!

Facebook
/BiggerPockets

Instagram
@BiggerPockets

Twitter
@BiggerPockets

LinkedIn
/company/Bigger
Pockets

Website
BiggerPockets.com